Modern Traditionalist Classical Music
Series Editor: Walter Simmons

Contributions to the series Modern Traditionalist Classical Music offer studies and assessments of composers and compositions, as well as classical music styles and techniques.

The Classical Revolution

Thoughts on New Music in the 21st Century

John Borstlap

THE SCARECROW PRESS, INC.
Lanham • Toronto • Plymouth, UK
2013

Published by Scarecrow Press, Inc.
A wholly owned subsidiary of The Rowman & Littlefield Publishing Group, Inc.
4501 Forbes Boulevard, Suite 200, Lanham, Maryland 20706
http://www.scarecrowpress.com

Estover Road, Plymouth PL6 7PY, United Kingdom

British Library Cataloguing in Publication Information Available

Library of Congress Cataloging-in-Publication Data

Borstlap, John.
The classical revolution : thoughts on new music in the 21st century / by John Borstlap. p. cm. --
(Modern traditionalist classical music)
Includes bibliographical references and index.
ISBN 978-0-8108-8457-1 (cloth : alk. paper) -- ISBN 978-0-8108-8458-8 (ebook) 1. Music--21st
century--History and criticism. I. Title.
ML197.B672 2013
781.6809'051--dc23
2012022714

The paper used in this publication meets the minimum requirements of American
National Standard for Information Sciences Permanence of Paper for Printed Library
Materials, ANSI/NISO Z39.48-1992.

Printed in the United States of America

Contents

Epigraphs

"During times of universal deceit, telling the truth becomes a revolutionary act."–*George Orwell*

"The end is where we start from."–*T. S. Eliot*

"There is nothing that music cannot do, as long as it remains music."–*W. A. Mozart*

"Everything that needs to be said has already been said. But since no one was listening, everything must be said again."–*André Gide*

"True art matters because it puts us in touch with what we really are, and enables us to live on that higher plane where freedom and fulfillment are given."–*Roger Scruton*

"History shows that evolution, however slow, is inevitable; but rather than allow it to take its course as passive spectators, oblivious or unobservant, we should play a conscious role."–*Pierre Boulez*

"Es gibt im Grunde nur ein Problem in der Welt, und es hat diesen Namen: Wie bricht man durch? Wie kommt man ins Freie? Wie sprengt man die Puppe und wird zum Schmetterling?"–*Thomas Mann, "Doktor Faustus"*

"Ein glückhaft Wünschen macht mich froh / Nach Freuden, die ich lang verachtet."–*Albert Giraud/Otto Hartleben (from Arnold Schönberg"s "Pierrot Lunaire")*

"'Torniamo all' antico: sarà un progresso."–*Giuseppe Verdi*

Acknowledgments

An explorative undertaking like this, however modest in scale, could not have been possible without long years of experience and reflection upon the practice of the classical music world and the reserve of contemporary music. Developing as a composer in these confused times requires a thorough understanding of one's motivation of every step, of the materials to be used, and of the position of art music in the modern world. A solid basis for that understanding was laid at the Rotterdam Conservatory, which offered lots of information but suffered from (a gradually discovered) bias on many levels, forcing a serious student of composition to follow his own lead; thus I was somewhat protected from the aggressive brainwashing of the "modernist revolution" in the Netherlands in the late sixties and early seventies, which also raged in the educational institutions. Characteristically, my early decision, after initial explorations in modernism, to return to tonality, cost me my final exam and the chance, upon a Dutch scholarship, to continue my studies abroad. It was my first encounter with the totalitarian side of modernist freedom: thou shalt be free in the way thou art *told*. The utter freedom that was supposed to finally enter an art form which was considered "restrictive" in the old days, erected a new taboo: the taboo around the impermissible return, in freedom, to the past. Fortunately, a year at Cambridge University in my thirties, made possible by a generous British Council Scholarship, made up for this unexpected outcome. The experience at Cambridge happened to be very fruitful, and this period fully confirmed all my observations of the workings of tradition (long misunderstood in the last century) and the nature of modernism, which was unintentionally nurtured by the head of the music faculty, Alexander Goehr, whose modest musicality was imprisoned behind the bars of a brilliant intellect modeled upon Schönberg's. Alexander, the son of Walter Goehr (who was a German refugee conductor and friend of Schönberg), was fed with the Schönbergian aesthetic from the cradle, inheriting a musical paradigm right from the horse's mouth. Understanding the Schönbergian heritage would mean understanding of the origin of musical modernism. This heritage was still close to tradition, which meant that Goehr—who felt much closer to this first wave of intellectualism than to the post-1945 avant-garde—did not want to cancel traditional concepts altogether. So, studying with him was as instructive and stimulating as it was revealing: musical composition not as a natural gift of expression and artistic imagination but as an intellectual craft with a consciously in-built "logic" and "consistency," an a priori structuralism suffocating any free impulses that might bubble up from the subconscious. Hence, Goehr's fascination for Debussy: the sublime "other" who *did* listen, and very attentively, to his subconscious, the unsuppressed "other," whom he found utterly attractive but of whom he did not seem to understand very much, and hence the sandy and constipated quality of his own professorial music where only very occasionally something *musical* would appear, like an unexpected and shy little flower in an immense desert. A clearer demonstration of modernism's fundamental misconception of music—and its explanation—could not be found, and it is thus no surprise that Goehr became the "father of modernism" in the United Kingdom, helping its "cause" within a performance culture still very traditional in nature. A couple of years spent at music agencies in Amsterdam greatly increased my understanding of the practical side of music life, especially the pressures which burden the careers of the "great names" and which help to explain their vulnerable narcissism and their indifference toward developments in the field of music, and even the occasional indifference toward the (traditional) music they perform, in spite of great talents of interpretation and expression.

Above all, I am grateful to the Dutch Ministry of Education, Culture, and Sciences, who—thanks to its financial generosity toward (from its point of view) a superfluous little luxury and its lack of expertise in matters of culture—supported the development of the Dutch modern music establishment, thereby creating an ideal biotope for modernist ideologies and mentalities, which could grow rank, shielded as they were from the limitations of the real world. It offered a perfect field of observation, in which avant-garde ideas from Germany and the United States (including the most virulent ones) fed the local compositional community, who now could stand out in protest against a "vile" society, which nonetheless was prepared to pay for it. The result was a small, interrelated world where the state's support made a mild imitation of the Soviet Union's Central Committee system possible, deciding on a national level and with the help of unverifiable criteria which composer was, and which was not allowed to be paid for his work, a system of control including party lines, infighting, excommunications, schisms, condemnations, aesthetic directives, financial fraud, and undreamt of supplementary incomes for the weekend hobbies of conservatory teachers. For the subject of this book, this system is worth a look, since it beautifully reflects the inner workings of the typical modernist mentality. Since the government rightly did not want to influence the course of music, they created a national financing fund that hired experts "from the field" to form the selection committees. Since these experts (modern composers and their performers) were themselves selected from the circles who received most of the subsidies and thus, had a vested interest in keeping the spirit of modernism free from "contamination" from the surrounding "bourgeois culture," the result was an appropriate expression of the total-itarian mentality that characterized the surge of "progressive modern music" as an expression of the times: composers who did not conform to modernist tastes were not paid for their work, even if there was a real demand for it in music life (because "bourgeois culture" could only be wrong). The result was that they had to find other means to sustain themselves, with all the burdens and limitations this implied. And "offi-cial new music," which could not function in the performing practice and in most cases was seriously lacking in quality of any kind, was funded generously in the hope of a future general recognition, a hope which was never fulfilled and will never be fulfilled. Because of a general lack of competence of the members, the selection committees of the music fund could not avoid serious blunders. In 2005, a Dutch composer made his five- and ten-year-old sons fiddle randomly at a keyboard, the result of which was—via a computer program—translated into a performable score for a collection of instruments, also randomly "chosen" by the kids. The composer offered the short piece to the fund, who not only paid €3,000 for it but complimented the composer with the quality of the piece's craftsmanship, adding that the idiom transcended his "regular work." An amusing short movie is on the Internet: www.youtube.com/watch?v=EkWyKMiTdzQ. So much for expertise concerning modernism. Such absurdism is only possible in the context of modernist ideologies. So, in a free, Western society, a totalitarian political regime was not neces-sary at all to create a totalitarian result in music life: the modernist circles were quite capable of organizing themselves in such a way, with un-founded "artistic criteria" determining which composers were "good" and could live by their work, and which were "irrelevant," just as in the Soviet Union, where a group of politically astute nitwits used nonsense criteria like "formalism" to create the best circumstances for themselves and to destroy careers of the competent competition. There exist exten-sive minutes of the meetings of the Dutch Composers Union (GeNeCo), which demonstrate the similarity between the bickering and infighting of its composers, trying to keep control over state subsidies, and the similar-ly abject intercourse among the bigwigs in the Union of Soviet Compos-ers, who had been consuming excessive state resources in pursuit of self-indulgent ends . . . an amusing and interesting treasure trove for future historians, providing embarrassing examples of how totalitarian thinking could be disguised as modernist "freedom."

Interestingly, in a recent court case, the Dutch music fund defended its artistic criteria by mentioning the work of John Cage as an example of truly "original" music, originality being a core criterion in the fund's evaluation procedure. To call Cage's work "music," and "original" on top of that, is a blunder of the first order: Cage was a joker like Marcel Duchamp, the "creator" of the famous urinal which he exhibited as a work of art in 1917 and with which he originated the deplorable fashion of "concept art." Cage is, to those outside of new music circles, nowhere taken seriously as a composer and rightly so—he was rather a decomposer. Both the Soviet term "formalism" and the Dutch fund's version of "originality," randomly used as a label for anything that committee members may happen to like at a given moment, can never be handled as a concrete criterium to assess music, since they can be interpreted in so many different ways as to be un-arguable. Both in totalitarian societies and in Dutch music life they are an ideal weapon in the hands of untalented people who like to sit in selection committees, covering-up their inadequacies with fake expertise and deciding what—in their eyes—is and is not formalistic or original. At the Dutch fund, the argument has always been: only our version is valid because we are entitled by the ministry to decide what originality means. It is a way of Humpty Dumpty–thinking, after the passage in Lewis Caroll's *Through the Looking-Glass*:

"When I use a word," Humpty Dumpty said in a rather scornful tone, "it means just what I choose it to mean—neither more nor less." "The question is", said Alice, "whether you can make words mean so many different things." "The question is," said Humpty Dumpty, "which is to be master—that's all."

With such a primitive interpretation of the concept of originality, *all* "artistic assessments" of such a state funding body for new music can be considered invalid. It is only with the emergence of institutionalized modernism that such incredible nonsense can find a foothold in society and receive government funding.

Also I am grateful for the hostility, abuse and indifference my work and ideas received in my country of birth, so that they could develop in quiet independence, unhindered by peer pressure, the usual competitive stimuli and the curious noses of malicious enquiry. The Netherlands are not representative of Europe as a whole, of course, but the underdeveloped sense of civilization permeating the country, resulting in its trendy "progressiveness" (in comparison with other European nations), has brought into sharper relief the destructive tendencies which lie at the heart of musical modernist ideologies. This is also in part due to the fact that new music has been more generously funded in Holland than elsewhere in the world (with the possible exception of Finland). The study of this little sound-art zoo, where modernist "philosophies" were given a free hand, has greatly contributed to my awareness of the link between the absence of *musical* talent and the idea of "pure sound," between a *kleinbürgerliche* populist society and the lure of a subsidized left-wing progressiveness determined to eliminate the unfair barriers of professionalism. The irritation resulting from various attempts to organize serious discussions about the problems of contemporary music and its wider cultural context confirmed my belief that most of the conventional "new music" not only struggles against the general indifference of the concert world, but more so with an inner awareness of the fragility of its artistic, aesthetic, and social position. Curiously, at the place where state support of new music is exceptionally generous, the insecurity about fundamentals is equally exceptional. Again, Holland is not Europe, but its distaste for history in combination with an optimistic outlook toward the modern world (especially toward "Big Brother" America), its practical skills, its cultivation of immaturity, and its happy freedom from the challenges of high culture, made it a perfect place to study the effects of the modern world upon the legacy of Europe's musical tradition which, also in Holland, has withdrawn behind the doors of a museum culture. The lack of a strong cultural elite, which could have inspired a closer commitment to civilizational values, gave more space to the excesses of contemporary music than would have been possible in other countries with a stronger presence of the past, where a new music establishment has not been able to *totally* control contemporary production and where there may be some space to allow for dissident opinions.

Currently the Dutch government is withdrawing its financial support for the arts in general, under the pressures of an unstable economy—which, however, is merely used as an excuse to fulfill the wishes of a populist right-wing faction, which has gained much support over the last few years. Comparable pressures are emerging in other European countries, but the drastic subsidy cuts in the Netherlands show what happens when a contemporary art elite exists exclusively by way of state support and in-crowd–pleasing ideologies without any artistic content. It provokes irritation with the uneducated masses, who in their ignorance project their displeasure over the entire field of art, including the old collections in the museums and traditional performing culture, seeing all this as an unfair waste of their tax money for luxury entertainments for the rich. The cuts have provoked an outrage within the artistic community, where fundamentally different parties, for once, found a common cause. But various protest rallies and loud debates in the media have not been able to soften the government's plans. On the contrary: the arrogant and offensive tone of many art elite members toward the populist enemy has deepened the hostilities. The result is the impression, as presented in the media, of three groups of protesters with different aims: the established institutions (who, in fact, suffer less reduction in their subsidy than the other parties), the empty-headed elite of new art and new music, and the irritated masses, as represented by the government. So, two different but intertwined forces of erosion–modernism and populism–attack traditional culture that could not possibly be blamed for both the vacuity of new art and the primitivism of the masses. Let all this be a lesson for all people responsible for the survival of culture in the entire West. Where modernism is institutionalized, civilization disintegrates.

    Last but not least, I thank the composers who had and have the courage to pursue various expressive ends in their work, often against great odds, and to explore the riches of the past while creating the beauties of the present. The contact with them personally and with their work has greatly contributed to the formulation and development of the themes which will be found in this book: from the UK, Robin Holloway, David Matthews, and Alan Mills; from the Netherlands, Hans Kox, Jeff Hamburg, and Joost Kleppe; from Austria, Wolfram Wagner (no family); from France, Nicolas Bacri and Richard Dubugnon; and from America, Reza Vali. Chapters 4, 5, and 6 first appeared, in a different version, as part of an essay "Recreating the Classical Tradition" in the collection, *Reviving the Muse*, published by the Claridge Press, UK, in 2001.

Introduction

Classical Music: A Dying Culture?

Can, in politics, a real revolution happen without bloodshed and without the following persecutions, purges, and suppression? In November 2009, anyone who followed the publicity around the commemoration of the fall of the Berlin Wall in 1989 would have sensed that this bloodless revolution, which began in Leipzig and then spread to other cities of East Germany, was a unique event with enormous long-term implications that are only beginning to be understood in these early years of the twenty-first century. The end of the Cold War opened up an undreamt-of future for Europe, and thus, will also have implications for its art, among which is one of the greatest achievements in the history of mankind: its art music. Still more time is needed for the mental walls to fall, however, walls which isolate and inhibit people, causing stagnation where new initiative is necessary. Much effort and courage is needed to rejuvenate the humanistic spirit of Europe as reflected in art music, which can be done by "stepping out of the box of received wisdom" and reassessing the possibilities of a new century.

The greatest challenge is the necessity of overcoming the nihilistic atmosphere of malaise, which is still hanging over this continent in spite of the material and social successes achieved in the period since the Second World War. The past half century is characterized by a spiritual crisis, a mental hangover, which can clearly be seen in most of its contemporary art and music, as presented in public space. This malaise should now belong to the past, to be overcome not with a naive and ignorant optimism but with a realistic wisdom honed by ages of experience and reflection, in particular the experience of the last century. Art music, as a symbol of human endeavor and aspiration, should be restored to its rightful place and level, and be carried again by the best of talents and the most constructive of ideas, to build a place where the creative spirit can dwell again and recover from the wounds of a confused and violent age.

This book is not a history, but instead explores the recently emerged idea of a restoration of the fundamentals of Western art music in contemporary composition. The approach is psychological and philosophical, connecting the subject with wider issues of cultural history (past and present) and the meaning of art. Specific and detailed technical analysis of new classical music and its fundamental differences from "official" new music of the last century should be left to future musicologists. First, the ground has to be cleared of the many misunderstandings still surrounding the notion of new music in order to arrive at a context where the subject can become transparent. Also, in this book there is a critique of modernism, modernity, and of the claims of atonal sound art to be music. In fact, the text sets out to undermine the two prevailing consensuses about "new music": first, the one circulating in the "new music world" that the average contemporary creation to which audiences are occasionally exposed is a normal development of the art form, and the second one, silently and broadly agreed upon in the central performance culture, which practices the "canonic" repertoire day in and day out, that *all* contemporary music is indigestible rubbish, or at least, inferior to traditional repertoire on a very fundamental level. One may ask, does it matter? Isn't the current pluralism—where anything goes, low and high, bad and good—a sign of a healthy, democratic society? Clearly it does, for the reason that the destruction of tradition, in all cultural fields, which went under the misleading heading of progressiveness in the last century, represents a disaster, an alarming signal with implications for our entire civilization because it deletes an important learning trajectory about the human condition. An immense treasure of wisdom, accumulated over the ages, is disposed of, as if it were a superfluous piece of ballast that would only hinder the flight into a glorious future, as if this future would not be inhabited by the offspring of the species, but by a newly created species: "modern man," free from the past and from his own nature. This may explain the often-sharp tone of this text—should one be tolerant of intolerance and incompetence, of downright destructiveness? Too much is at stake to allow for a soft approach. Art is not an isolated little garden for highbrow entertainment; it reflects what is going on in a much wider context. Here, it seems appropriate to freely paraphrase the art critic Roger Kimball: the assaults on tradition represent one front in a much larger war, a war over the tenor and shape of our culture, over our shared understanding of what the Greeks used to call "the good life for man."

In the confusion and inferiority of what goes for contemporary art and contemporary music in public space, a reflection can be seen of a process of decivilization, a slow process we can observe all around us under the glamorous surface of the modern world. We are witnessing an assault on a culture, on a way of looking at and valuing the world and our place in it, and what is presented "officially" as contemporary creative production is often a direct result of this erosion. Something went totally wrong in the last century's art and especially in its music, an awareness which only recently began to slip into the minds of the artists directly committed to the art form: its composers. The Austrian scholar Otto Pächt noted in his *The Practice of Art History* (1999): "When we travel, we first make sure we get on the right train. In art history, people tend not to do this — and then they are surprised when they find themselves at an impasse, or at the wrong destination."

The same can be said of many "established composers" of the last century, who — imagining that they populated the only possible train into the future — ended up in a deserted ruin. Amusingly, this state of affairs is often better understood by the bystanders. A couple of years ago, an Arte TV documentary showed sound artist and conductor Pierre Boulez explaining the developments of twentieth-century music. When Debussy was discussed (and played in the background), visions of fertile, leafy summer landscapes in golden sunlight were shown. The sound art of more "progressive" composers, however, invoked black-and-white images of derelict industrial zones where the wind blew some bits of torn paper (from discarded scores?). With an unerring sense of reality the producers set Boulez, when reciting the great achievements of modernism, in the middle of a factory ruin, overgrown with grass.

The fundamentals on which European music rested since its early beginnings, eroded during the twentieth century, and led to a sundering of "new music" from the central performance culture into a very different context. As a result of this, the central performance culture — once a flagship of European civilization — has gradually turned into a museum culture, a thing of the past, and for many people no longer, through contemporary creation, in a direct sense related to the modern world. But in these intervening years an increasing number of composers attempted to revive art music as the expressive art it once was, to restore new music as a true successor to the ages of the "great repertoire," reconnecting with certain artistic values that lay at the heart of European music from its earliest beginnings, and which have, as a natural basis, been lost during the political, social, and economic changes of the last hundred years.

The word "natural" in this context cannot be taken for granted and needs some elucidation. Art, including art music, has always been a human construction, in the sense that civilization is a creation of the human mind and answers an emotional and spiritual need. The creation of art is, in this sense, a natural characteristic of the human being. Art can be found in prehistoric times, as soon as the human species had developed enough to be able to organize itself into more or less social communities. The word "spiritual" also needs some clarification: in this book the concept of "spiritual" is meant to describe that part of our mental life which aspires to transcend the material world with its demands, and tries to create a higher form of inner life experience, including intuition and religious inclinations, as well as intellectual exploration.

The need to explain these terms in the context of art music, in an effort to reassure the reader that they are not used here for superficial snob value but as substantial matters, shows how much Western society *as civilization* has eroded. Before the onset of modernism, discussing expressive, emotional, or spiritual factors in contemporary music was perfectly normal and widely accepted. The creation of art, which is fundamental to any civilization, has always been a normal activity in a society; it addresses the need to have deeper questions about life and the world expressed and explored in a mental space, one which is separated from the concerns and pressures of daily life and the forces of nature. It is a recent achievement in an evolution of millions of years, and in that sense, a climax in the development of life on this planet. It also means that art is deeply psychological: it is the *meaning* of art that is crucial: that which is communicated, though the "message" need not be straightforward and clear; its aesthetic stylization—necessary to lift it above the material world—both underlines and blurs its meaning, rendering it ambiguous, multilayered, and multi-interpretable. This complexity is, at the same time, ensuring different and ever-new interpretations, creating durability and continuity over long and different periods.

The different layers of meaning in a good work of art (i.e., a work which meets the requirements that in a flourishing culture may be expected from art), can only partly be understood consciously. In this sense art can be compared with the symbol, which is a sign, a ritual, or an event that contains more than can be understood at its rational surface. The work of art and the symbol have much in common, but the element which makes up the difference between the two is the aesthetic aspect: to function, the symbol does not necessarily need to include aesthetic elements, but the work of art is merely a symbol if it expresses itself without aesthetic concerns. The aesthetic element is crucial to art. It is its "language," it is the level where style, expression, and construction come together in unity.

After this detour, it will be more clear at which level the erosion of European art music becomes visible. It is the decreasing understanding of the inner life of art and of the human being, as projected through various channels in public space. The central performance culture is part of this space and is increasingly considered—from outside of this culture—as an isolated, marginal phenomenon. Often, stories of "the death of classical music" are reported by the media: audiences are dwindling and aging; young people have lost contact with tradition; dullness of performing, routine in programming, and incompetence in composing, plus the lack of music education, undermine the art form in general; media coverage and reviewing are shrinking both in quantity and in quality; and so on. However, news about opera houses and orchestras getting into trouble, stories about bankruptcy, funding scandals, and complaints about fees of superstars, have always existed in music, and seem to structurally belong to music making—the fertile mix of glamour, emotionalism, ego celebration, spiritual aspirations, and extraordinary artistic achievement—seems to foster irrational and egoistic behavior in a climate of vanity and intrigue. But the sound of "a dying culture" seems to have grown both in range and intensity, together with a general feeling of malaise throughout European society concerning its culture, its cultural identity, its values, and its future in a globalizing world where mental darkness is increasingly finding voice and violence.

From the Second World War onward, and in spite of the cloud of the Cold War, Western European nations were calmly and steadily growing toward each other, with the perspective of some kind of "unified Europe"; peace, wealth, and security were relatively quickly achieved, thanks to the loyal and generous support of the United States. Only an ongoing process of clarification, discussion, balancing out of interests, and further bureaucratic structuring and differentiation, would eventually bring about something like an ideal society, the apotheosis of an ongoing process of civilization. That this was to some extent just wishful thinking is shown by the gradual erosion of educational systems and generally of civilized values in the Western world, which found (and still finds) an alarming expression in the media, increasingly giving space to a primitive popular culture, and also too often in exhibitions of modern art which can be considered showcases of what cultural elites are supposed to consider appropriate and worthwhile. The apparent stability of society, in combination with an increasing "democratization" of taste and manners, provided—under the influence of nihilism—a perfect soil for what always in human history has been the heralding of barbarism: psychological malaise, decadence, the loosening of constraints on the all-too-human lower instincts. But for a while, at least in physical terms, Western Europe seemed a relatively quiet and safe world which would continue to be so forever. Then came the surprise of the bloodless revolution of 1989: the fall of the Berlin Wall, the dissolution of Eastern Germany followed by the quick German unification, the end of the Cold War with the disintegration of the Soviet Union and the liberation of Eastern Europe from communist domination. Unexpectedly, Germany found itself at the heart of a new Europe, a position with great responsibilities and in a minefield of suspicions and anxieties. But, at the time, it seemed a big step toward the ideal of a unified and reborn continent where peace and wealth would reign.

The September 11 attacks on New York put a drastic end to the feeling of physical security in the entire West: suddenly an abyss opened up. A problem territory that—though noticed before—had become directly threatening to Western economic and political strength and hegemony. In Europe, elites became aware of the presence of millions of immigrants from Muslim countries, bringing with them a culture more traditional and identity-conscious than modern European culture. The failure to create a "European Constitution" in 2006 only underlined the real state of affairs: the European political and economic project was in a crisis, adding to a general feeling that European civilization as a whole was stagnating, with discussions popping up about the "immigration problem" and "national identity." "Canons" of historical and cultural figures and facts were drawn up, TV docudramas were created about subjects of national history, plans were devised to more strongly regulate integration of immigrants, while opposition to immigration and the irrational fear of an "Islamization" of Europe led to increasing support for extreme rightwing political parties. Terrorist attacks in Europe added to tensions along the many fault lines of society, both in a political sense and in cultural terms. The politically correct and often complacent dream of a multicultural society appeared to not quite match reality. It was a vision cherished by an elite which had not had much contact with the realities of mixed—and often poor—immigrant communities in the cities. The fashionable "cultural relativity" of the elites, which gave "equal status" to the different cultures within European societies, hindered Europeanization of immigrant communities, groups who often tended to isolate themselves from Western society. This, combined with the erosion of faith in the idea that it was possible to win over peoples from different backgrounds to a common set of secular, humanist, enlightened values, created a serious problem for Europe's cultural identity: neither immigration, nor Muslim integration appeared the real stumbling block, but the lack of conviction in an open, secular, humanist project, which would also be attractive for non-European people. And on top of all this, the enduring economic crisis that began to undermine the West in 2008 forced elites to rethink their liberal, capitalist society, and especially the values underlying the system. It had the additional result in Europe that the integration project of the European Union suddenly was jolted out of it bureaucratic complacency.

What has all this to do with our musical culture? The answer is this: that serious European musical culture—and by extension, serious musical culture in the entire West—is much more than the entertainment for which it is often regarded. It is a powerful expression and symbol of Europe and the West as a civilization. In its humanism it embodies the values that lay at the heart of our society, values which are formed by the Enlightenment and the interplay between its ideas and reactions to them. From this process, an idea of a pluralist, secular society was born, which can be considered a higher form of civilization than mono-cultures that only can be maintained through suppression, exclusion, and state-steered characterization. But a pluralist society can only exist if a fundamental framework is accepted by all members, a framework which creates an underlying unity but offers enough space for variety.

"Culture" in the anthropological sense is a broad term that refers to the general characteristics of a given society; it is about "how people live." "Culture" in the traditional sense is the life of the mind, of the mental space in which human life and the world are reflected, processed, and where possibilities and opportunities are explored in thought experiments and finding a stylized realization in the arts. Art music until modernism—being an abstract art form that does not directly refer to physical reality—had always related to those strata of the human psyche that were less accessible to the reflective intellect; it is closer to the motors of the human being—like intuition, instinctive drives and existential hopes, needs, and anxieties. But as an art of active creation, as opposed to re-creation (interpretation in performance in the 20th to 21st century), serious music seemed to have died and been replaced by very different ideas about music. The result is the now general division of musical activity into the central performance culture on one hand, almost exclusively based upon a repertoire from the past, and the "new circuit" with "contemporary music" on the other with specialized ensembles, festivals, and performing venues. The difference between these two cultures is so fundamental that one can speak of two distinctive paradigms with a repertoire type that attracts two different audiences who both have specific expectations. In the current argument, it will be shown that here we have a musical culture with works created in the past and perpetuated in the way of a museum, and a totally different art form, which can be best described as "sound art" or "sonic art," a new art form developed in the course of the last century as a fruit of modernist thinking and based upon a fundamental break with past practices and past artistic and aesthetic values. Sonic art is often totally dependent upon state subsidies, and thus living a rather artificial life, while the musical museum culture, although partly subsidized as well, can (still) count upon much wider audience support. General developments in Western society as a whole have led to a marginalization of both the museum culture and sonic art in public space, which is increasingly dominated by popular culture with its instant entertainment. Although not dead, it cannot be said that both art forms are living a healthy life. Much effort has to be done to reconnect the museum culture to contemporary society and to have its correct place in public space restored. Also, sonic art has its legitimate place in the totality of cultural activity, because modern liberal society can and should include different art forms of different quality and meaning. But most important is the attempt to rejuvenate the musical museum culture as a *contemporary* art form through the revival of the classical tradition—classical in the widest sense—which reduces the museum character of the existing repertoire, establishing a continuity with its tradition, enriching it with new creation, reflecting both upon the new and the old, and reconnecting it with the modern world and its pressing needs for civilized values and aspirations.

In this book, "classical" is not referring to the restricted style period of the late eighteenth century, but to the European tonal classical tradition as a whole, in the same way as we look at "Indian classical music" as different from the modern world with its modern entertainment which also makes inroads upon that long-standing and high-minded tradition. Musical modernism is understood as the type of "music" that first emerged in the works of Schönberg from opus 23 onward, in which he used the principle of twelve-tone composition for the first time, which is the first realization of serialism. This system thinking made a "music" that was not organized according to the laws of tonality possible; its organization is materialistic, without an ordering of sounds through to-nality (the receptivity of which is "hardwired" in our brain) and thus, inaudible. Instead of the term "modernism" as describing a forward-looking mentality (applicable to any art which consciously wants to be "progressive"), in this text it means, when related to music, a sound art without the organizational possibilities of tonality and thus, a new form of art which makes use of sound but is not music (thereby sundering itself from the European musical tradition and creating a space of its own). Its characteristics will be further explored in chapters 2 and 3.

The following argument is meant for everybody who is involved in the music world, be it as programmers, promoters, performers, compos-ers, critics, members of advisory committees for subsidy bodies, listeners with more than the usual interest in music, and music lovers who feel uneasy about the future of classical music in general, and about the pecu-liar world of "new music" in particular. It is especially meant for profes-sionals who feel some confusion about new classical music, because it mars their views of music history as received through their education, and who may mistakenly suspect the return to more traditional values as a trend toward "conservatism." That new music can also sound like "old music" comes to many people as a surprise, given that they have become used to expect a certain "modern" sound of new compositions, which is supposed to relate them to the modern world. But it is not the world which dictates a style to its artists. It is the other way around: it is the artists' imagination which determines the style of a period, and history shows that individual interpretations of a more general notion of style can differ to a great extent. The motivation of the "new classical compos-ers" can be compared with the drive of artists in the Italian Renaissance, who tried to recapture the qualities and styles of Antiquity, artists who felt no inhibition to take their examples from the past, because they were confident enough that their interpretation could eventually equal the old-er art and would leave them enough freedom to develop in personal directions. It would have been absurd to ask from an Alberti, a Bruneles-chi, a Raphael, or a Michelangelo, that they "express their times"; they *were* of their times, and by creating with personal authenticity and sincer-ity, they shaped the artistic identity of their era.

Misunderstandings surrounding new classical music often result from an outdated notion of what constitutes "the modern world" and from the misconception that history consists of a linear narrative, which is a serious distortion of reality. History is irregular, capricious, full of unforeseen happenings and trajectories unexplored. In a wider context, progress can be achieved in some fields, for instance in the development of modern liberal democracy and the welfare state, but only in science can a notion of progress be defined in a concrete way. Art is not a concrete, objective activity as science is, and thus the history of music cannot be compared to the history of science, which indeed is linear, propelled by theoretical speculation but developing on the basis of proven fact: a concrete form of progress of knowledge in terms of quantity and quality. But the notion of "progress" is meaningless in art.

Also, the text takes Europe as its center of attention, not because America would be less significant to the subject, but because American societies (north and south) are culturally so different from Europe. After all, classical Western music as a high art is European in nature, so the present argument has its consequences for America as far as it is a European import, and in relation to the specific American perspective. Namely, historical perspectives and notions of cultural identity have a different meaning in a culture which is a relatively recent creation, and which is based upon immigration from other cultures. Of course there have been valuable contributions to art music from the Americas, but they have a different meaning as compared to the developments within the heartland of its origin. A truly multicultural society like the United States creates a different mentality in relation to art and its meaning for the community, often stimulating a more practical than theoretical approach. This is already shown in the fact that new classical music (i.e., new music rooted in the tonal traditions) is already partly accepted in the orchestral world of the United States, where hardcore modernism has mostly retreated to the defensive bulwarks of music faculties in the universities; practical questions, not philosophizing, seem to operate in American concert practice. With some generalization one could assume that Americans are more likely to trust their instincts as to which music works and which does not, while Europeans allow their intellectual apparatus to decide for them first rationally which music *should* work: the ongoing and pointless European efforts to get modernism accepted in the central performance culture have always been doomed to fail, and are still failing, and will continue to fail, but this does not deter its advocates, who still hope for success against the massive evidence of the contrary. Such stubbornness is only possible where the problems of contemporary music are exclusively seen from a rationalistic point of view, and all the psychological, aesthetic, emotional, and spiritual elements are undervalued, suppressed or simply not noticed.

It will be shown that musical culture, on one hand, and sonic culture, on the other, are two different worlds of experience and that friction emerges where sonic art claims to be music, thus impinging upon the fundamental artistic values of music. Only where these values are eroded or have disappeared can sonic art give the impression that it is a natural development of music; where sonic art is accepted and celebrated as music, music has truly died and, with it, the values it embodied.

The text is not built up in the way of a logical argument, but paints on a broad canvas through the presentation of interrelated short observations and meditations, organized around the different themes, which together form the subject, so that gradually the entire picture with the connections between the smaller units becomes visible. Some bits may, in terms of meaning, overlap; for instance, it is not possible to describe in a straightforward, linear way what music *does*: the characteristic ambiguities and subtleties of the art form would then be lost. Music is not an art form which can be argued in the way mathematics can be argued. This does not mean that all we say and think about music is condemned to remain purely subjective. There is a good reason to assume that reality, inside and outside ourselves, contains territories which have objective reality, in spite of their seemingly ephemeral nature. The sensitive and intelligent reader will be able to relate the picture thus painted to his or her own experiences and will find in the overlapping or impinging of his or her own world with the one as described in the text a reason to consider and (further) refine his or her own opinions concerning the subject described.

Readers who have sometimes wondered why greatness in musical composition seems to have gradually disappeared in the twentieth century may find an answer in these pages, as well as the possible solution to the problem that caused its demise. Programmers in the central performance culture may find good reasons to take the classical revolution seriously and see it as a welcoming injection of new life into a museum culture and, especially, an inspiring and much-needed chance to mobilize audience interest in its developments and thus, in classical music in general, which in its turn can only be good for orchestras, opera companies, ensembles, and soloists in a context where populist claims threaten their existence.

ONE

The Classical Revolution: The Shock of the Old

Contemporary composers who try to regain something of the glory of the musical art of the past do not form a coherent group. They do not form a specific movement, but reflect a tendency, felt more generally over the last few years in Europe, to see "progress" and "modernity" less and less as determining factors in society and increasingly consider notions of *value, meaning, tradition,* and *cultural identity* as possible orientation points. The reason behind this tendency is an increasing awareness that "modernity" is not the only, and certainly not the most important, drive behind any development that improves human life. While an erosion of civilization is becoming more and more visible, there is a growing awareness that with the emphasis on materialistic and technological progress, and with the neglect and indifference toward the culture of the past, much precious human experience may be lost, experience which could be of importance in this period where, on a deeper level, there is (in Western civilization as a whole and certainly in Europe) no sense of direction. This awareness translates itself in Europe, on a political level, in the increasing popularity of rightwing parties (unfortunately in some countries also in primitive populist movements), and in a renewed interest in conservative world views, which should not be understood as a retreat to outdated belief systems but as a sign that much leftwing thinking, as developed since the 1960s, has come under critical scrutiny. Many "progressive" ideas from that time are now seen as having overstepped some boundaries of common sense, which resulted in the careless throwing away of concepts without which a civilized society cannot be sustained. This does not mean that the original idealism of socialism has been discredited, but that some of its later forms are now appearing more like aberrations than fulfillments. The same could, however, be said of some extreme forms of

1

conservatism like the so-called "neoconservatism" in the United States which, together with a rampant and uninhibited globalizing capitalism, threatens culture as well as nature in every place where it gets a foothold. Postmodern thinking, with its poisonous fruits of cultural relativism, foucaultism, and deconstructivism, has infiltrated many university curricula where they, instead of merely extending some existing traditional ways of higher learning, often *replace* modes of thought which have proven their importance and worth, based as they are upon long experience and processes of trial and error. On another level, there is a link between the erosion of education of the masses and their inclination to leave more and more responsibilities to governments, as if the state would be the best repository of efficiency in running human life. It is therefore not surprising that the increasingly bureaucratic organization of European societies shows — helped by modern information technology — a tendency to totalitarianism, as if not much has been learned from the experiences of totalitarian regimes in the past. In this melting pot of mental confusion, the long European tradition of humanistic thought, with roots in Antiquity and subsequent flowerings in Renaissance and Enlightenment, stands out as a rock of wisdom and understanding of the human condition in a sea of triviality and materialism, thus offering orientation points for the task ahead of European/Western civilization: restoration of the best that this tradition can offer, whereby valuable insights of later experience can be integrated and further developed.

So, with the search for workable values, the concept of tradition has become important again. As long as it is understood as a flexible and living *process* which develops itself by continuous interpretation, it is not a "conservative" notion, an attempt to merely try to construct an imitation of something old. Seen this way, a new form of tradition in society — culture and thus in art music — is neither conservative nor progressive in the old senses. It is a sign of rebirth, of a possible *renaissance* of the best that Europe has to offer. It will be clear that such a concept can easily be misunderstood because notions of "progressiveness," "conservatism," and "traditionalism" have served in the last century as banners for political interests. They were related to circumstances which now have drastically changed and thus have lost much of their original meaning and appeal. Given the many problems which confront Western civilization as a whole, it is clear that a fundamental reform is needed to make its survival and further development possible. In Europe, this means a reorientation upon its values and its nature, which involves a reflection upon its past and the lessons that can be learned from it. It is to be hoped that some form of workable and valuable *cultural identity* of Europe can be found and formulated which can function as a mental framework in which the current problems can find a fruitful and sustainable solution.

Also, the presence of so many non-European immigrants who need to integrate into European society stimulates a stronger awareness of the nature of the society in which they are supposed to integrate. If Europeans have only a vague and incomplete awareness of their own cultural values, there is not much to culturally integrate into, apart from the most basic mundane skills. Mere "freedom" cannot compensate for the loss of a culture that was "left behind" because it was "outdated," in order to make place for a modern world in which everything was to be shaped anew. "Freedom" in itself is a meaningless word if not related to "from" and "toward." The result is an emerging debate about what European/Western civilization is, or should be, and old themes concerning the Enlightenment, Christian religion, civil society, secularity, and the like have become important issues again in public debate because, in the present confused globalization with all its political and economic implications and side effects, nothing less than the future of Western civilization is at stake. And Europe as it has been, can no longer be taken for granted: it has become an idea to be discussed. Art, including music, is part of this discussion.

In the visual arts, many painters returned to figurative styles as composers (somewhat later, as usual) began to reconsider their own past: tonality and communication instead of materialist constructivism. In art music, the first "thaw" came from California in the form of minimalism, or, for a better term, process music, which restored continuity, narrative, and a simple form of tonal harmony. From Eastern Europe, Arvo Pärt appeared with his religiously inspired process music, close in spirit to that of the Middle Ages. American process music and Eastern European spirituality was widely followed and imitated, but both trends cannot be considered "classical" in relation to the central performance culture. They established themselves at the margins of this culture but (due to their use of tonality) with a direct and living link to it and in opposition to the circuit of "established modern music" which still followed the norms of postwar modernism as formulated in the '50s and '60s (mixed with milder, "postmodern" derivations). Seeing that tonal process music provided a bridge toward the central art form, various composers began to explore its underlying energies, experimenting with reviving tonal styles and elements of tonal languages, mixing them in new combinations. This trend is a form of "classicism" in the sense that exploration of the past might lead to new forms and new developments. The emergence of process music can convincingly be called a revolution, as can the new form of classicism be called a classical revolution.

For the term "revolution" to be justified, there has to be a dominating force against which the new art form is in rebellion. Process music rebelled against the complexity, inaccessibility, and plain acoustical ugliness of atonal modernism, which—with the help of academe and state subsidies—had been widely established as "the" way "the" Western music was "developing," as if art music were a single communal project led by the avant-garde, in the way a political party or an army is led (and from where the term stems). New classical music is rebelling against the now eroding modernist establishment but also takes distance from process music because of its restricted range of expression and structure. Many listeners who have sat through a process music performance—for example of John Adams's opera, *Nixon in China,* to name one of its better examples—will at some moment have felt the question bubbling up as to the reason for all these endlessly repetitive patterns, effects without a cause in the subject or action. Purely absolute, nonreferential process music suffers from the same handicap. The continuously repeated fragments form a kind of "sound wall," which is not so impenetrable as it is with modernism because the sounds are often quite nice, but the expressive possibilities are very limited and its effects wear off in the long run. Its main interest is to be found in the organization of its surface, in the ingenuity of its patterns, and the effectiveness of its scoring. The return to a full-blown tonality is, of course, a decisive step in process music, often stimulated by pop and world music and therefore reconnected to more general modes of music making and perception than is offered by modernism. But to regain the expressive range as demonstrated by premodernist tonal music (i.e., the classical tradition)—classical in the widest sense and with its last great representatives in Dmitri Shostakovich and Benjamin Britten—one has to rethink the notions that have led to modernism, the model of progress in music, the concept of tradition *an sich,* and most important, the idea of contemporaneity, since a return to the European classical tradition in the sense of a *literal* repetition of what has been, would not be possible and anyway superfluous. But the new classical composer does not want to imitate, and sees as his or her challenge to make a real, personal contribution of valuable works which could, in principle, in due course, take their place in the repertoire of the central performance culture without disrupting its fundamentals, as so often is experienced when occasionally a modernist work is performed in the context of an otherwise normal symphonic or chamber music concert. There are good reasons to consider such an experience as an intrusion from outside, from a fundamentally different sphere, as we shall see in chapters 2 and 3. (Many programmers are fully aware of this when they put a new piece right at the beginning of an otherwise normal program, the notorious OOMP—Obligatory Opening Modern Piece—which fulfills the obligation "to do something new" and to get over it as quickly as possible in order to arrive at the real stuff of the concert.)

Something like a "classical revolution" seems a *contradictio in terminus*: how can a new "classical music" be revolutionary? That is, overthrowing some old order and creating a new one, with all the heroic overtones and narratives of struggle and victory that the term implies, when the norms it advocates are already general practice in the central performance culture? Is new classical music not just a form of conservatism, a concession to a petrified and commercial practice? If this were so, one would assume that new classical music is welcomed with open arms by the regular orchestras, opera theaters, and classical chamber music ensembles, given the fact that most new music is—in that world—generally considered indigestible and ugly, and irrelevant because of the abundance of excellent and well-tried works from the past. A new music that fits seamlessly into the framework of a well-worn repertoire would offer something new without the usual problems of communication: it would seem a sure bet on success and one would expect the programmers to roll out the red carpet to new classical music, but this is not the case. In the musical museum culture, it is generally assumed that "new music" is for specialist environments like festivals and concert series by specialist ensembles for special audiences, like the "authentic music circuit" with its baroque ensembles made up of period instruments. This makes *any* interest in whatever new music in traditional concert practice seem superfluous. (Occasional performances of new, modernist music by regular symphony orchestras are mostly the result of an isolated feeling of obligation, mixed with a bit of heroic image making—fighting for the new is a matter of personal courage—and sufficient funding which can compensate for the prospects of losing audience attendance; it is hardly ever based upon a success with performers and audiences.) On top of this, new classical music of authentic quality does not *literally* sound like old, repertoire-like music; it may sound familiar and at the same time, "strange," like something unusual said in a known language. Thus, it may initially create some confusion: what is this, where could it be placed, what does it say?—which is a normal reaction to *anything* new. Of course, new works need repeated hearing and if the first impression is positive, (i.e., it raises interest and trust in the capacities of the composer), new hearings further strengthen the experience. New classical music is *new music* in all respects, but its unusual aura may upset fixed expectations even if, in comparison with the usual "modern music," it speaks in an accessible, expressive language. Also, the emergence of a new classical music is such an unexpected and, in fact, a potentially spectacular phenomenon, that many programmers simply do not believe it is possible: in direct comparison with the established repertoire it is considered inconceivable that *contemporary* composers, born in a much more trivial world, so different from the one where this repertoire stems from, could emulate the works of Britten, Shostakovich, Mahler, or "purer" music like Ravel's, Debussy's, or Stravinsky's; the impossibility of the appearance (in terms of talent) of a "new" Mahler, Debussy, or a "new" Mozart or Beethoven, is deeply ingrained in the museum culture (therefore, the recent emergence of a first-class composer like Nicolas Bacri is not generally recognized as a phenomenon of the first order: "it could not possibly be as good as it sounds"). Programmers have studied music in the last century when music history was mostly presented as a line from the past to the present and on which the development toward atonality and modernism was projected as the result of some historical inevitability. From this conventional point of view, a new classical music could only be either *kitsch* or an irrelevant pastime of reactionary eccentrics.

Kitsch is the imitation of an expressive gesture, a cheap imitation that remains on the surface. It is not *meant*, as authentic art is meant, it is false and for that reason it creates the unpleasant "yuck" sensation in people whose sensibilities are trained in the experiences of high art. As Roger Scruton says in his *Modern Culture*, from the modernist point of view,

> . . . you can turn back to figurative painting, to tonality, to classicism —
> but you will only be *imitating* these things, never actually *doing* them.
> You can *make* the old gestures; but you cannot seriously *mean* them.
> And if you make them nonetheless the result will be kitsch — standard,
> cut-price goods, produced without effort and consumed without
> thought [emphasis in original, p. 92].

Since kitsch in this sense is about expression, it is a psychological category. But an artist will only *not* mean an expressive gesture, if he does not believe in the possibility of authentic expression, or if he is — due to a lack of talent — not capable of such a thing. But if — in terms of talent — an artist *is* capable of authentic expression which he could mean, in which he could believe, but *rationally*, because of his upbringing and education, he believes he is locked up in the narrow present moment on the line of historical narrative, he cannot allow himself to mean an expressive gesture. This is what modernist brainwashing and myth making has brought into the world of art: the idea that it is not possible that an artist could mean an expressive gesture which has come down to him through history and with which he could identify himself with integrity. It is exactly on this point where the narrow historicism of modernist ideologies has destroyed tradition.

The Hungarian sonic artist György Ligeti expressed this feeling of being "locked up" in the present moment on the line of history in his famous saying where he expressed that he felt imprisoned between, on one hand, the past, and, on the other, modernism. Eventually he found a way out of his dilemma by using elements from both the European past and from African cultures, always in a modernist way of structuring material, as he considered himself a constructivist. (Talking about his music he said, "It is not for the audience, it is not even for me, but a thing in itself.") Indeed, his "music," and also his later works, "say" what a "constructivist" does with the sound material: it is channelled through a mincing machine to get it fragmented, splintered, pulverized, and then somehow put together again — but the notes do not connect, in spite of the gestures. The resulting material is not something living, organic, breathing, but comparable to sand, gravel, or the concrete of modernist buildings — life has been ground out of the sound. Also where he tries to write melodically, as in "Melodieen" (which is one of his best works), the fundamental problem shows itself all too clearly. The "lines" are not *melodic* lines because there is no musical energy "moving" from one note to the other as in music. The notes are short or long horizontal, disconnected lines as in a Mondrianesque painting. They do not have the characteristic and expressive curves as we find them in Gregorian chant, Bach, Beethoven, or Debussy, where the notes are bound by tonal forces and an unerring feeling for expressive beauty.

When contemporary artists see through the nonsense of modernist kitsch-phobia, they can feel free to identify with expressive tools of past periods, interpret them according to their own personal tastes, and thus make them contemporary. In music, it is only possible to distinguish between authentic expression and kitsch on the basis of listening experience; the more one has heard authentic expression, the better one can recognize kitsch, although it is impossible to objectively prove the difference to an inexperienced person because the qualities of that distinction remain in the emotional and aesthetic realm. However, it can still be argued that the music of Pärt is authentic, while Gorecki's is kitsch, as the quasi protest-music of Louis Andriessen is typical '60s kitsch, and most film music, and—yes—quite some passages in Mahler, are kitsch, however much he attempted to elevate them by putting them in quotation marks and tried to make them sound ironic, and however his advocates try to elevate him to a 20th-century martyr saint of the modern soul. Also much of the music of Richard Strauss is kitsch, next to much that is genuine and authentic. The phenomenal opera *Salome* thanks its artistic success to the appropriateness of the kitschy passages which are—intentionally or unintentionally—functional and totally effective in expressing plot and characters.

Another accusation that new classical music often receives is that its composers merely try to please audiences by using the languages it has got used to. So, the motivation of trying to renew traditional musical languages, which is genuine and legitimate, is translated into opportunism and commercialism. In cases where this can be confirmed, the music can indeed only be kitsch; however, the use of more familiar musical languages will make comparison with the great repertoire possible so that this kitsch can easily be detected. The legitimate motivation of using older languages has, in this way, a built-in protection against abuse. Behind the accusation—which mostly comes from the modernist camp—lies the assumption that dissonance, complexity, and inaccessibility (mostly resulting in aural ugliness) somehow are signs of sophistication, while accessibility and beauty merely demonstrate naivety or worse: primitivism. In reality, to be sophisticated and complex in an accessible way is dependent upon an artistry far superior to anything sophisticated that could possibly be produced within modernism (as, for instance, the subtleties and sophistication of Beethoven's chamber music amply prove). And as far as commercialism is concerned, it can be argued that as commercialism is a mentality driven primarily by the lust of money, the territory where this lust is blatantly a most obvious drive is exactly the subsidized circuits of established modernism: it is *there* where the money flows, and the fact that it is the state that is the client and not the audience or some private maecenas, does not diminish its character of real commercialism: the trading of goods for the money of the client with the aim of making profit. Modernism *is* basically meant for the authorities, as represented by the subsidizing bodies, because the musical audience as a natural party to the art form has been written out of the paradigm of modernist thinking—of which the above-mentioned quote of Ligeti is a telling example. As we shall see in chapters 2 and 3, modernism is, in its deepest nature, a totalitarian, top-down structured belief system, artificial, antihumanist, anticivilizational, and unintentionally an appropriate expression of the totalitarian societies which have disrupted Europe in the last century. Ironically, instead of an expression of the free world, there is no better commercial *Reichskunst* than modernism.

The idea of kitsch, as used in modernist ideologies, refers to notions of expression which were seen as outdated and irrelevant to the modern world: in the modernist *grand narrative of history*, musical expression was something not universal, but time bound to historical cultural circumstances. And indeed, modernist "music" does not know kitsch because there, the entire dimension of expression is absent. It does know cliché, of course, which is the empty, conventional repetition of established gestures and procedures that even within a modernist context have now become utterly trivial. (If a modernist work begins with one long note, bet on it that the second is either a minor second, a tritonus, a major seventh, or a minor ninth: the four most popular modernist intervals which represent disconnection.) New classical music is open to the critique of kitsch as any music is, but it is absurd to put the entire genre a priori in that category according to a misconceived idea of history. Kitsch and expression are fundamentally different things.

Expression, in all kinds of variety, has always been an important ingredient of art music from Gregorian chant onward. Even the strict and formalistic baroque fugues were meant to provoke excitement, which may be of a different kind than, for instance, the excitement created by an operatic *lamento* aria, but excitement nonetheless. So-called "neo-classical" works by Stravinsky, who claimed that music was incapable of expression, are expressive, as the masterly *Violin Concerto* and the *Symphony of Psalms* amply attest; only, their expressivity operates under the surface of a quasi-formalistic classicism that gives the emotional intensity an indirect quality. To state that expression is just an inessential bonus laid upon the real body of music, and as such a product of the "decadent" nineteenth century, is a blunder of the first order and a distortion obviously meant to bolster the aesthetic position of the postwar avant-garde in a hostile, traditionalist environment which did not want to give up what it rightly felt to be at the heart of the art form. The modernist idea of music history as a linear narrative was meant to be a justification, but also a prescription, as Pierre Boulez claimed in the 1950s: "Any composer who has not felt—I do not say understand—but felt the necessity of the dodecaphonic language, is USELESS."

The unfolding of history is not prescriptive but a natural process of actions and reactions of individuals and groups. It does not follow one single line but myriad lines, in which only with hindsight may certain patterns be discerned, which are often open to different interpretations (this is the reason why there is, next to music history, also a history of music history). The linear narrative of modernist music history excludes the possibility of renewal and development of alternatives and is therefore *reactionary* and *conservative* through and through, as the accusation of kitsch toward new classicism shows. The history of modernity is not the same as the history of culture, and the blurring of the two in modernist ideologies should be seen as a barrier to understanding artistic reality, which can only be assessed on the basis of our experience of works of art from all periods and places.

Therefore, the aesthetic position of "new classicism" has to be seen in the light of deep-rooted misunderstandings as to the nature of music history and the concept of modernity. It is an invitation to open the box in which a majority of programmers and artistic leaders in the musical museum culture are still thinking, oblivious of the chances which are offered to them. And it is in their interest that audiences can experience this new development, because new classical works are a rejuvenating injection into the existing repertoire, underlining this repertoire's living presence not only as works from the past but also in its progeny in the present, thus establishing a direct link with the living and inviting commitment and discussion. It is the strongest possible justification for considering classical art music in general as a culture which is fundamentally relevant to the Western world. The implications for the position of classical music in general within society are obvious.

To summarize, new classical music has to battle against four categories of resistance:

1. the conditioned prejudices concerning "new music" of performers, programmers, and artistic leaders in the central (traditional) performance culture who think *any* new music is "bad" and "ugly"
2. the mind set of policy makers in government institutions who are responsible for state subsidies for new music, which is dominated by models of "progress" and "modernity," and the need to protect the "avant-garde" from perishing in a "hostile" commercial environment
3. the "modern music establishment" with its specialist ensembles, festivals, and radio producers, who form a network of financial

interests because the genre is almost totally state subsidized; competition from a fundamentally different new music which can be
integrated into the central performance culture undermines the
justification of its existence

4. the music critics who, after decades of modernist propaganda and
professional embarrassment about wrong assessments in the past,
have cautiously accepted "established modern music" on its own
terms

One could also formulate these categories in terms of taboos:

1. the taboo that new music can be beautiful, expressive, and meaningful
2. the taboo that new music does not need special protection because
it can be both sophisticated and popular
3. the taboo that new music can be organically integrated into the
central performance culture
4. the taboo that modernist sound art can be bad, conventional, reactionary, and superfluous like any form of music

So, within the confusion of values (artistic and otherwise) in modern
European/Western society, a restoration of art music is simply a "back to
normal," an attempt to reconnect with a glorious past with the hope and
confidence of continuing artistic creation on the highest level, celebrating
the European creative spirit in a new context. Given the consequences of
the greatest rupture in music history since its beginnings, the break with
tonality, which in the last century destroyed a precious tradition, this
restoration is in fact a revolution since it requires a thorough rethinking
of a form of twentieth-century "received wisdom," which still dominates
musical life both in the central performance culture and in the "modern
circuit." It is a battle against conventional thinking and above all against
a misunderstood modernity. It is a struggle that has to be won by argu-
mentation, focusing upon facts and experience, the importance of classical music for society as a whole, and, above all else, the artistic quality of
new classical works.

And yet, this revolution is going on already for two decades, quietly
and decently, carried by individual composers who independently of
each other discovered some very basic truths about Western musical culture and set out to delve into the hidden layers of history, searching for
the well that fueled ages of remarkable creation. Can the term "classical"
be dynamic, or is it always referring to something static, something ven-
erated, accepted, with the veneer of past glories? It depends upon the
interpretation of the term "classic" or "classical." The Italian Renaissance
was a rebirth—or so it was thought at the time—of the glories of the
civilization of Antiquity, and it was a very dynamic force, giving birth to
the modern world. It had nothing static about it and was indeed a revolu-

tion that, after various earlier attempts, resulted in a broad flow of aston-
ishing creativity which only petered out with the rise of modernism in
the twentieth century. In the current argument, "classical" is meant to be
understood as exactly such a dynamic concept, as an idea of re-creating a
great art form, one of the important gifts to humanity; "classical music" is
thus understood as a term covering Western art music from its earliest
beginnings with Gregorian chant until the onset of twentieth-century
modernism.

TWO

The Fallacy of Moderism I: The Truth That Dare Not Speak Its Name

Before abolishing something, it would be wise to first stop to consider its merits. However commonsense such prudence seems to be, in the development of art music it has not always been an easy imperative to carry out because merits can be obscured by prejudice, circumstantial debris, and all the usual human inadequacies. It can be argued that during the last century, the break with tonality was the greatest rupture in music history because what was given up was not something at the surface level like style or a type of expression, but the very fundamentals of music as an art form. The loosening and, finally, the giving up of the basis of art music was an impoverishment of immeasurable and dramatic scope, ruining a precious tradition that had been an important cultural flagship and raising walls everywhere in the musical world. It also had something absurdist about it, like a new type of high-tech banqueting where all attention is invested into new forms of elaboration in the use of cutlery, plates, glasses, serviettes, and ritual, but where no actual food is served.

Ironically enough, this abolition was welcomed by enthusiastic generations of people who thought that the basis of art music was something that was better dismissed since this act opened up a wide panorama of possibilities on the level of sound material, which seemed to more than compensate for the loss of aesthetic and communicative capacities. This disappearance of a craft, which had developed and been refined over the ages, made "musical composition" more accessible than it had ever been. With the barriers of "irrational" qualities removed, practicing the art of composition became available to people with materialistic and rationalistic skills but who did not possess the musical gifts that can make the materials of music live and breathe. Unfortunately, by now it has become obvious that the idea that modernism was just a further stage of Europe's musical tradition was not progress, but rather, a tragic mistake. This will become clear if we look deeper into the basis of music: tonality. It can also be concluded by examining the arrogant and noncommunicative mentality of composers of atonal, modernist music, composers who show no understanding of the fragile relationship between the composer's individual imagination and the listener (who, after all, is supposed to be the "other" with whom the composer's creations are supposed to be shared).

Of course, there is often a "time lag" between new music and its understanding by audiences. This does not mean that if there is no understanding of a new work, it is *therefore* a brilliant, forward-looking piece. Also, time lags could be quite long in periods before the reach of modern media; however, after almost a century of modernist music (if we count from Schönberg's piano pieces opus 23 from 1923 onward) and, after the Second World War, half a century in the best possible conditions in terms of media information channels, supported by virulent intellectual propaganda and generous state funding, it can be concluded that music without tonality does not belong in the central performance culture if audiences in this culture, generation after generation, cannot accept it as music. After almost a century of rejection, the audiences' resistance can no longer be explained away as the result of a "conservative attitude" and "unwillingness to learn new things," as the recent firm establishment of the music of Shostakovich in the central repertoire, with its often unpleasant, nihilistic complexities, proves. It is in the music itself where the real problem has to be located, and this problem has destroyed the fragile relationship between the contemporary composer and his audience as it had existed before. We will see that tonality is the bridge over which communication can pass, the sense of musical communication being an instinctive recognition of the inner workings of music's energies. Blowing up this bridge is a deed of cultural terrorism, the damage of which will be very hard to repair, certainly so in times when serious music as a whole is no longer considered an important cultural phenomenon in the public space.

Ernst Roth, director of the famous Viennese publishing house Universal Edition from 1928 to 1938, when he moved to London, where he worked at Boosy & Hawkes, knew composers like Schönberg, Szymanowski, Berg, Webern, Stravinsky, Bartok, and R. Strauss from direct and close contact while publishing their works. Being not just a businessman but also an erudite connoisseur, equally at home in music, painting, and architecture, he saw the birth and early development of modernism, as it were, happening under his nose, and could make well-informed comparisons. He was also knowledgeable about the post-1945 avant-garde movement. In his very readable memoirs from the 1960s, with the double-edged title *The Business of Music*, which explores both the business and artistic side of music publishing, it is clear that he let himself not be blinded by modernist utopianism, understanding from the inside the importance of the power of music to communicate. He predicted that if serious music was to evolve further along modernist lines, the interest of audiences would dwindle and eventually be lost, and that even a later return toward a more traditional attitude would hardly be able to win back the audiences' goodwill: "Even if a symphony in pure C major could be written today the public, indifferent to all types of new music, would reject it."

Unfortunately, in a general way, this still holds true today. As any orchestral or opera programmer or concert promoter knows, a contemporary name on the program will almost certainly mean a reduction of ticket sales. The notions of "unknown," "contemporary," and "modern" are like red warning signs for something indigestible or uninteresting, and even the composers who cannot be blamed have to suffer from their effect. A comparison with premodernist musical life, when new works by Wagner, Mahler, Strauss, Debussy, Ravel, Stravinsky, Bartok, and so forth, were anticipated with curiosity, shows the immense change which has taken place in audience expectations. Now the worst excesses of modernism have receded and much new music has acquired a less inhumane sound quality, but the mistrust and indifference is still very deep. Modernism did not only destroy goodwill for its own creations, it destroyed it for any other new music as well.

Modernism, as formulated both theoretically and in terms of works of art at the beginning of the last century, was not meant to kill off tradition. As Roger Scruton writes about early modernism in his *Modern Culture* (1998):

> The first effect of modernism was to make high-culture difficult: to surround beauty with a wall of erudition. The hidden purpose was twofold: to protect art against popular entertainment, and to create a new barrier, a new obstacle to membership, and a new rite of passage to the adult and illuminated sphere. To those whom modernism excluded, the movement seemed like a betrayal of the past. Tonality and tunefulness in music; the human image in painting; the pleasing dignity of metre and rhyme—even the homely comfort of a story well told—all these ways in which art had opened its arms to normal humanity were suddenly rejected, like a false embrace. To the modernists, however, the past was betrayed not by modernism but by popular culture. Tonal harmonies had been corrupted and banalized by popular music; figurative painting had been trumped by photography; rhyme and metre had become the stuff of Christmas cards, and the stories had been too often told. Everything out there, in the world of naïve and unthinking people, was kitsch. Modernism was not an assault on the artistic tradition, but an attempt to rescue it. Such was the surprising thought expressed by Eliott and Schönberg, and their eloquence transformed the high culture of Europe.

With hindsight, it can be concluded that in so doing, modernism unintentionally killed the essence of the tradition of high art: its humanity; and in
its constructivism and ideologies of progressiveness it tried to take on the
appearance of science, which was, after all, to become the most spectacular endeavor of Western civilization. But art, of course, is not science,
which is based upon fact, research, and theoretical speculation, which is
verified by proof. Art is subjective by nature and thus operates on quite
another level. As the art historian Ernest Gombrich said in an interview
in 1994:

> Objective assessments about art are not possible. In art there are de-
> bates, but objective arguments are not possible in that territory and on
> this point art is different from science. The reason for this is not that
> judgment in art would merely be a matter of taste, but because our
> experience of art is so closely intertwined with our culture and person-
> al development. (Dutch newspaper *NRC* 28/10/94: "The unexpected is
> trivial")

Music became a caricature of science and of what was perceived as progressiveness: a line of history projected into the future—and the most
important yardstick of "value" of "musical works"—thus reducing an art
form that was an expression and representation of the inner life of man to
a merely materialistic playground. Also it provided the tools of contempt
for creations that did not meet the requirements of avant-garde conditions; music from the past was belittled as a product of people who,
unfortunately, did not have the knowledge and understanding of the
highly endowed present. (A residue of this quasiscientific thinking still
exists in the way new classical music is sometimes treated: looked down
upon as something lacking the sophistication of modernity, and its composers seen as naïve children who have not as yet understood that the
earth is not flat.)

In music, it was Arnold Schönberg who took the first step toward the
drastic materialist intellectualization of the art form that would have such
following in the last century. To be able to do that, he had to somehow
break away from the fundamentals of the old tradition that he thought to
be corrupted and outdated. Upon developing his twelve-tone music, he
created the first form of a sound art that, at first, seemed to have most
elements in common with music, except the basis which made art music
possible at all: tonality. Much ink has been spilled over the question of
what music actually is, and what tonality is. A couple of books that
explore this territory can be found in the bibliography at the end of this
book. For our subject, it is sufficient to conclude that tonality is the relationship in terms of resonance that exists between separate tones, a relationship made possible by the physical phenomenon of overtones. In
every tone, other tones softly resonate; above the fundamental tone these
overtones are in the order of octave, fifth, again octave, third, again fifth,

and smaller intervals which spread out in an increasingly diffuse and faint range at the top. The closer the overtone is to the fundamental, the stronger the connection and the stronger the resonance caused by the amplitude ratios of sound. As Alex Ross formulates in his *The Rest is Noise*, paraphrasing Hermann von Helmhotz:

> As the waveforms of any two simultaneous tones intersect, they create "beats," pulsations in the air. The interval of the octave causes a pleasant sensation, Helmhotz said, because the oscillations of the upper note align with those of the lower note in a perfect two-to one ratio, meaning that no beats are felt. The perfect fifth, which has a three-to-two ratio, also sounds "clean" to the ear.

This still holds as an apt explanation of the natural, physical resonances which are possible between different notes. This type of relationship is like a force of gravity which pulls a sound toward its fundamental tone. In a musical work, a fundamental tone could be compared to the vanishing point in figurative painting: it is the point to which all the lines of perspective and all the objects in the "virtual" space of the image are related, thus creating the effect of space in an otherwise flat surface. Our brain immediately "recognizes" spatial depth where in reality there is only a flat surface, because our capacity to interpret these lines of perspective as depth is hardwired in our visual sense. In a comparable way the fundamental tone is the focus of all the relationships that operate in a piece of music at a given moment, and since music moves in time and all the different tones move according to the parameters of melody, harmony, and rhythm, they continually shift their relationship toward the fundamental tone, in continuously varying degrees of distance and strength of connection, thus creating the effect of energies moving along between fixed, less fixed, and floating positions. The result is what metaphorically could be called an "aural perspective" in which the force of tonality, with varying intensities, continuously focuses upon the fundamental tone: a "musical space" comparable to the quasi-physical space created by perspective in a figurative painting. The gravitational force of tonality makes the scales—the basic materials of music—possible and the simultaneousness of different tones forming a coherent unity: harmony. And it makes direct communication possible via the ear and brain, which are related to the natural phenomenon of overtone series: the difference between an octave and a second, is immediately aurally perceptible even to the most unmusical person. Our perceptive organ and the physical nature of sound are closely interrelated, as our whole body is part of nature's overall "design." Compare this to the reactions by pet animals to music or visual art: apparently, they only see the material presence of a painting and only hear the sound a musical work makes; they are not capable of seeing "into" the image or hearing "into" the music.

The differentiation of tonal relationships, a territory gradually explored over a couple of hundreds of years, created an impressive range of complexity. For example, the "gravity" which binds the two tones of an octave together is much stronger than the force which creates a relationship between the tones of a third, and the combination, which makes up the interval of a second is so far removed from the fundamental in the overtone series that the two amplitude ratios "clash," they create a "rubbing" effect which can be used as a psychological tension, which can resolve into a third (which has a much less "clashing" quality), or used as a coloring, depending upon context. Every combination of different tones can have specific qualities in terms of tension or character ("color"). These differences of correspondence can create the impression of energies flowing from one type of intensity to another and can thus be used by the composer to create a musical narrative that gives the impression of movement, and thus a musical rhetoric is made possible. The total field of pitches, from very high to very low, offers many different relationships between the tones. In higher registers the interval of a second is less experienced as a "clash" than in lower regions, because in the lower acoustical depth the overtones of a fundamental tone are stronger and can thus more easily "clash" with other tones or overtones. This variety in relationships offers ample opportunity for playing with the differences in tonal tension and pitch, like the interplay of consonances and dissonances in different contexts and in different musical styles. Thus tonality guarantees infinite ways of combination, of styles, of types of expression, and this order that inhabits the physical phenomenon of sound is the "instrument" through which the unfolding of music history—with its impressive artistic achievements—has been possible.

But the tone *system* of Western art music is not exactly the same as the interrelatedness of natural overtones: it is an adaptation, an artificial structure within which the natural interrelatedness—the tonal "gravity"—can function, binding tones together, but with enough flexibility to make all kinds of tonal complexity possible. As is generally known, since the eighteenth century, the tradition of tuning keyboard instruments was developed with a slightly adapted tonal interrelatedness, in which small deviations of tuning made it possible to modulate more easily from one tonal area into another. By "stretching" the alignments of the tuning system and "equalizing" the tone material, it became more flexible because individual tones could be related to a wider variety of other tones at the same time. The result is the chromatically even tonal field where the pull of octaves and fifths—the intervals most strongly related to the fundamental—are still much present, but the binding of smaller intervals is slightly weaker. Tonality is *not* this equalized, flexible system in which the music can go in any direction, but is the "gravitational force" created by the relationships of octaves and fifths, gradually weaker in smaller intervals, a natural force operating *within* this human construct. In a tonally, relatively simple tone system, like the medieval modi, this force was equally operating and, because of a purer tuning, closer to the natural overtone series. With the development of the chromatic field the finer tuning of smaller intervals was lost, but this was more than compensated for by the enormous range of expressive possibilities of combination and modulation which it opened up, possibilities which could develop, intensify, and refine the gravitational force of tonal relationships.

Tonality—the binding force created by nature—is a flexible and ambiguous force. It is a field of energy and not a "structure" or "system," and when seen as such it will become clear that the idea of trying to create an art music *without* tonality is inherently absurd. Tonality is not a manmade structure but a natural phenomenon, "tamed" within the tonal system of modes, scales, and harmonies of European art music. The ear, like all of our senses built to relate to the surrounding physical reality, automatically picks up the aural "perspective" created by the "gravity" of natural overtones, and the cultural conditioning on which art music is based is thus itself based upon a natural phenomenon, which is part of the world around us and which is built into our physical system.

The physical nature of tonality makes a directly experienced emotional impression possible, and it gives music its almost tactile quality, which is experienced through the physical sense of hearing and received as direct, emotional stimuli. The intellect can be conscious of the process of stimuli reception and the reactions to it, but this is not necessary for music to have its effect; hence the success of music therapy in the treatment of mentally or physically disabled patients, where the order that is inherent in music has an ordering influence upon the human being, both mentally and in relation to the motor nerves. The physical nature of tonality is experienced by the listener through the physicality of the hearing sense and its unraveling by the brain. In the mind of the composer, this physical quality is closely related to other sensual stimuli; hence the stories of composers being stimulated by nonmusical things such as landscapes, the visual arts, emotional experiences in themselves not related to music, and the like.

In 2010, the Dutch cultural philosopher and painter Lennaart Allan published, together with two other authors, a remarkable book in which the developments of modernism in the visual arts and its philosophical/theoretical background are analyzed: *Not Everything Is Art* (Aspekt Publishing, Soesterberg 2010; unfortunately as yet not available in English). Allan describes all the important art theories from Romanticism until and including postmodernism, advocating a return to representation—*mimesis*—in the visual arts, on sound philosophical and aesthetic grounds (*mimesis* is an old complex Greek concept, denoting a combination of imitation, representation, and imagination). He remarks that the theory of representation, which has its origin in Aristotle's notion of representation, not only of external phenomena but also of human emotions and characters, (i.e., the whole of external and internal reality as experienced by man) is not merely plausible because of its long tradition, but fully convincing because it is a result of how the human mind works. Aristotle postulated that the human being is a "mimetic animal" who learns by imitation. On the surface, Allan says, this is obviously true. But the human being has, next to his or her analytic and logical mind, the capacity for what Allan calls "mimetic thinking": this is the way of thinking manifested in representations, metaphors, models, parables, stories, analogies, examples, and resemblances, which are used to express oneself and to convince others, but which is also used to obtain an insight into reality.

In music, mimetic thinking is the source of creation and invention: composers are stimulated by visual experiences (nature, the visual arts), by imagery evoked by texts (poetry), and/or the wide range of various amorous experiences; saturated with "tactile" stimuli they can "mould" the sound material in their mind as if it were a physical substance, as experienced by the other senses of seeing and touching. This is not some kind of magic but the normal act of a highly gifted imagination expected from talented people. The craftsmanship which is necessary to transform the imagined musical "visions" into a practicable score requires much rational thinking, but this process is—with the really great talents— steered by the other process of "tactile" imagination, from which the radiance comes in what was called in former times "inspiration." To describe it in an "old-fashioned" way: the spirit of the inner image was embedded into the score.

The character of real life experiences thus went into the music. The refinement and elegance we find in eighteenth-century music is a direct reflection of the environments of nobility and court, which were the "trendsetting circles" in those times. Beethoven made a daily walk in the leafy surroundings of Vienna, armed with a sketchbook to be filled with the musical ideas he "picked up" there. Chopin lived an almost artificial existence in the overrefined salons of Paris, which made him feel badly displaced even on a picnic walk. Berlioz threw himself into one emotional storm after another, strongly reacting to *any* stimuli from the world. Wagner—in exile in Switzerland—regularly made trips into the Alps, which gave him a sense of superlative grandeur until then unimaged in music, while the luxurious fabrics with which he decorated his home— shimmering silks and deeply colored velvets—found their counterpart in his colorful orchestration, of which the "tactile" quality was further stimulated by smell and touch. He composed *Parsifal* in a study damp with perfume, stroking a fur cloth on his lap at moments of reflection (talking about *Parsifal's* instrumentation, he mentioned "layers of clouds" that combined and separated). Brahms was a typical healthy "outdoor person," feasting on the air of woodland and meadows. Debussy intensely absorbed the experience of natural phenomena and the fantastic imaginations of poetry and dreams, collecting objects of art and visiting exhibitions. Mahler almost exclusively composed in a little hut looking out over the mountains. Richard Strauss intensely studied art history and always visited the local museums when on tour. Stravinsky wrote his scores as if they were graphic art works themselves, with different colorings inspired by his interest in painting. In his pre-dodecaphonic period, Schönberg often painted himself (quite badly, but that is not the point). Messiaen's hearing was so closely wired to his visual sense that he heard chords as "real" colors; and so on and so forth.

All these "tactile" stimuli went into the music of these composers because of their strongly developed mimetic thinking, which gave them the possibility of handling the sound material in a way that was comparable with the visual arts, turning it into instruments of expression. (It may be no coincidence that two of the noisiest scores in the repertoire, Strauss' *Salome* and Stravinsky's *Sacre du Printemps,* were composed in a room the size of a broom cupboard—cases of musical overcompensation?) In "music" without tonality—sonic art—however, the material is treated in a rationalistic way, which can be compared with painting without representation: an art form distanced from mimetic thinking, and thus leading toward abstraction, distanced from the world and from the tactile/mimetic experience of the human being, focusing upon "pure" sound material. The colorings of sonic art, however sophisticated and pleasant they may sometimes be, thus have no mimetic meaning. They merely represent themselves, are not transformed into a musically meaningful inner space created by tonal relationships, and thus cannot overcome the limitations of decoration (one of the flaws that diminishes the quality of much of Messiaen's music). It is thus no coincidence that the later works of Mondriaan have a close psychological and emotional resemblance to the later works of Webern.

The phenomenon of tonality is a *condition sine qua non* for the creation of music and for giving music its expressive qualities. It is the most effective tool in the hands of a composer with real musical talent. (Of course, tonality does not *create* music, but is the conditional requirement for the creation of music.) In the visual arts, the greater the artistic gift, the more the artist will be inclined to use the mimetic means as developed by tradition, because they will give him the best and the most varied opportunities. A new Raphael or Leonardo will be found among the new figurative painters and not among concept artists. It is the same with music: the greater the talent of a composer, the more he or she will be drawn toward the resources of tonality and its stylistic ranges. A contemporary composer with the talents of a Beethoven, Mahler, or Debussy will not be found among the "composers" who think that tonality is a superfluous and outdated tool or that they can infuse their work with the drab confections from pop or world music, jazz or film music, without restricting the artform's potential. Given the immense richness of past achievement, a really great talent will try to emulate, not to destroy or deny it.

The conventional historical narrative of the development toward atonality is one in which composers under the urge of romantic expression stretched the "system" to such an extent that it finally burst. Wagner was the first composer who undermined tonality, and in his wake Mahler and Strauss, who further demolished tonal coherence and Schönberg, who finally drew the consequences and "courageously" left tonality altogether. However, it is incorrect to conclude that tonality was outworn and outdated because of this: by including tonal, but more tense relationships further removed from the fundamental tone, the aforementioned composers *intensified* tonality, in a musical language of increasingly powerful expression, until Schönberg went to the very edge of what is musically possible. Crossing over the natural limitations of tonality can only work as a means of expression within a context where these limitations are still in place, as in some passages in Strauss' *Salome* and *Elektra*; crossing boundaries in a territory where there are none is impossible. Instead of wisely stopping at the edge of the abyss—as Strauss and Mahler did—Schönberg jumped into it, not happily but in despair about his own personal life, his perspective as composer, and the reality of the world around him. What happened in the course of the nineteenth century was a change in the way music was *organized*: classical principles of form (which were based upon stable key areas) gradually changed into other ways of organizing musical expression (more "open," more ambiguous, often as if floating in a chromatic field), which went together with a different approach toward the function of tonality. So, if anything was "undermined" it was the classical structural systems, but not tonality.

The expressive intensity of Wagner's later operas (*Die Walküre, Siegfried, Tristan und Isolde, Götterdämmerung, Parsifal*) was achieved through a superb handling of the difference in tension between consonance and dissonance, for instance by long withholding resolution of a dissonant chord, as in *Tristan*, whereby energies were sometimes intensified to an almost unbearable degree. This would not have been possible if tonality as a gravitational force had been "undermined" and in some way diminished. Tonality makes expression possible and the inner space of music where the musical energies can form their various flows. Wagner's handling of tonality is much more ambiguous than in earlier music; in his operas surface phenomena float upon undercurrents of long-term tonal energies, where the fundamental tone is often, as it were, hidden from direct experience and indirectly steering the flow of the music. The distance to the fundamental tone, which makes the music more dissonant or/and ambiguous, does not "undermine" the relationships of the tones to the fundamental tone, but differentiates them; it is a refinement and often a reinforcement. A "hidden" fundamental tone does not mean it has less effect or power—in Wagner quite the opposite.

A work in which the interplay between consonance and dissonance, and the dynamics and power of an extended, intensified tonality can be experienced in an almost drastic way is the first movement of Mahler's posthumous 10th Symphony, the famous Adagio in which, at the climax, an extremely dissonant chord still finds a resolution in a consonant concluding passage. In the same movement, Mahler creates another unusual tonal effect: a purely tonal minor chord in a dramatic orchestral tutti which, after much wandering through ambiguous tonal territory, works as a *psychological* dissonance in spite of—or thanks to—its utter stability: the drastic and secure sound of nearing catastrophe in which he specialized. (It was Mahler, and not the "Second Viennese School" or any music following in its wake, who perfectly expressed the *Zeitgeist* of the twentieth century in its angst, nostalgia, and feelings of alienation, fragmentation, and loss, not as an "objective representation" but as emotionally experienced.)

Schönberg's so-called "first period of atonality," or "free atonality" (i.e., as yet not bound by a consciously structured system, opus 10–22) is, in fact, still tonal in the sense that the gravity of the fundamental tone is still present—albeit at the edge of what is possible (and sometimes going over the limits). The tragic and fragmented intensity of *Pierrot Lunaire* and the expressive force of the *Fünf Orchesterstücke* derive their effect from a traditional, tonal background to which the music is still referring, however desperately and on the verge of ultimate breakdown.

In the first 15 minutes of the monodrama *Erwartung*, the mental darkness of psychic catastrophe is perfectly expressed by shadow-like, spooky music, in which tonal centers are continuously—for very short moments—suggested, as if the music hints at invisible objects in the dark, never fully presented and thus perfectly suited to the stage situation: a woman lost in a dark forest or park and in a mental state alternating between panicked observation, emotional confusion, and hysterical hallucination. Obviously this is an end point of what music can do, and later in the work the quasiromantic gestures, floating in a directionless space, lose most of their expressive effect because of the lack of contrasting material and focus points—they sound lachrymose and whining, not tragic. Schönberg always presented his development toward atonality as a recognition of a historical necessity, as if he were the martyr of musical progress as emerging from the internal dynamism of the tonal system in the late nineteenth century, drawing the consequences which Mahler and Strauss were not capable of following up. But now we know that this morbid and depressed music is related to a marital crisis, with his wife eloping with his friend, the painter Richard Gerstl, who committed suicide in a dramatic way when the wife returned to her husband. This was in 1908, when Schönberg was working on his second string quartet (opus 10) with a soprano in the third and fourth movement, based upon poems of Stefan George, in which the music leaves the ground of more or less traditional harmonic function and floats in a (still tonal) desolate space. The mentioned *Fünf Orchesterstücke* and *Erwartung* followed in 1909, after which Schönberg further explored a style in which despair and alienation reign supreme.

In the long run, this free-floating despair without focal points was nothing for a systematic mind like Schönberg's; despair *with* focal points was more to his liking. Shortly after World War I, he designed his system of composing with twelve tones, dodecaphony, a first attempt to bring order in the cloud, organizing tones not according to the force of tonality—which would, from his point of view, have been a "compromise" with the "outdated" aspects of tradition—but following an arithmetic ordering, which looks very clever on paper but is imperceptible to the ear, a system further developed by later composers after World War II into the ordering of all parameters according to arithmetic principles: serialism. In serialism, factors like duration of notes, rhythm, and dynamics were "ordered" according to numerical principles, which is—if possible—even less perceptible. (A thorough analysis of tonality, atonality, and serialism can be found in Roger Scruton's monumental *The Aesthetics of Music*; see bibliography.) Schönberg saw his twelve-tone idea as a progressive development of art music and hoped that in due course it would replace the "system" of "outworn" tonality and could thus save the classical European tradition from triviality. Of course this has not happened and the irony of Alban Berg's attempts to still write tonally while trying to obey twelve-tone rules, which his music did not need at all (as his brilliant and tragic opera *Wozzeck* shows), and the sheer ineffective ugliness and constipation of Schönberg's attempts at nontonal classical music in twelve-tone-style, illustrate the confusion at that time (the first quarter of the twentieth century) about the nature of music and its place in a modernizing and quickly darkening world.

Schönberg's mental world bristles with fundamental misconceptions—for instance the idea that a chord in itself can become trivial by overuse, or that a dissonance is something that can be emancipated, or that a collection of notes in its inversion or retrograde maintains its musical identity, or that in musical space location is irrelevant to identity (as if factors of high, low, left, right would have no effect upon the character of the musical material). A chord is just basic material and derives its significance and expressive meaning only within the context of a musical structure; a chord in itself cannot be "trivialized" by overuse. It is the context which makes chords, melodies, and gestures trivial. If this were not so, we could no longer suffer to listen to Bach, Mozart, or Beethoven with their recurring "common chords." Similarly, dissonance is dependent upon context: two "clashing" notes (because of their "rubbing" overtones) can work as a tension to be resolved or as a striking coloring which is enough in itself; in a style where "clashing notes" means dissonance, emancipating this effect by no longer resolving tension does not emancipate the dissonance but cancels it: dissonance only works in a context where it can resolve into consonance, as the later operas of Wagner overwhelmingly demonstrate. Changing such important characteristics of note collections, like playing them upside down or backwards, as a rule, *does* change the collection's identity because the effect is different. A motive may sound well in its original form and awkward in its inversion, and part of the "old" art of polyphony is to find other forms of the same note collection which sound as well as the original appearance; Bach was, of course, a master in this. (To call the contrapuntal writing in atonal Schönberg, Berg, and Webern "brilliant"—as has been suggested so often in modernist ideologies—is nonsensical, because in an idiom where differences between consonance and dissonance is cancelled, *any* combination of notes is more or less OK; counterpoint becomes a real challenge in a tonal context where all the forces of harmony, degrees of dissonance, and pitch determine the result.) And contrary to what Schönberg thought, in musical space, location is everything, and even in the classical style the recurrence of a theme on another pitch in a recapitulation—mostly not more than a fifth removed from the original pitch—changes the nature and expression of the music. Location is crucial because, in the lower regions, overtones clash more than in the upper registers and thus, pitch defines the sound coloring of the music.

Because of Schönberg's tortured and misconceived thinking—which shows a serious problem with the realities of musical substance but presented with rationalistic pedantry—lesser-gifted people with equally problematic musical insights could comfortably take over these ideas and develop them further for their own interests. Musical composition always includes much of intellectual work, but all rational structuring is merely the means by with a *musical* vision is realized. To take the structuralist aspect of the art form as its center is like putting the horse behind the cart. Eventually, this mentality would disrupt the art form from "the inside"; would "explode" it into the fragmentation and incompetence, which can be heard in specialized "modern music festivals." There is this amusing story of the summer visit of Poulenc and Milhaud to Schönberg in the 1920s, when they were having dinner while the children of the dodecaphonic master were playing in the garden. Hardly had the soup tureen been placed on the table that a ball splashed through an open window right into it, generously distributing the contents over the participants, upon which Schönberg with grim humor stated, looking intensely through the vermicelli hanging over his bald scull: "This is what I want to do with musical life."

Meanwhile it should not be forgotten that Schönberg had the musical gifts of a genius, as his earlier works attest, of which his *Chamber Symphony* opus 9 deserves special mention. Here, different stylistic fields—including "old-fashioned" Brahmsian tonality—find a marvelous one-off symphonic synthesis in which the expressive forces of tonality are utilized to the utter limits, but differently from Mahler and Strauss: its compact rhetoric is closer to Beethoven's (the only time he was able to emulate Beethoven's concept of dramatic sonata form). If anything, this work proves that here a way was shown in which his music could have developed: a return toward tradition enriched with a personal and effective handling of dissonance, maybe something like Strauss but with more structural panache and direction. In fact, Schönberg later sensed something of the kind, regretting in an interview in the 1930s that he had not followed up this style, because he felt that there still were many possibilities to be explored in that direction. (The German psychologist Julius Bahle: *Der musikalische Schaffensprozess. Psychologie der schöpferischen Erlebnis- und Antriebformen*, Leipzig 1936, Konstanz 1947; quoted in Willi Reich: *Arnold Schönberg, oder der konservatiuer Revolutionär*, Wien/Frankfurt/Zürich 1968, Verlag Fritz Molden, p. 307.)

That even gifted musicians can fall into the trap of Schönbergian myth-making is demonstrated by one of the few conductors who show something like an interest in the nature of music itself apart from their own career. The well-known conductor, Daniel Barenboim, a man with great musical qualities and an otherwise independent frame of mind, occasionally explores philosophical questions of music in the context of the broader culture, as in *A Life in Music* (2003, Arcade Publishing), where he offers meaningful insights into the nature of this high art form and its place in the context of the modern world, an art which he rightly understands as an embodiment of humanistic, civilizational values. Yet, in a recent TV interview, he explained "the development toward atonality" in the conventional way described above, underlining "the historic inevitability" of atonality (without explaining the "why" of the inevitability).

This view explains the oddity of Barenboim conducting works by Boulez, which embody the total repudiation of everything he professes to believe in — it is like helping the hangman lay the rope around your own neck. Similarly, in the text of a January 2010 London concert program, Barenboim compares Beethoven and Schönberg as two similar heroes who created "irrevocable consequences for the future of composition" (thus using the very jargon of modernism), and this would make "their absolute value different from other composers" (hear the totalitarian tone ringing in the distance . . .). According to Barenboim, "Beethoven's movement toward ever further disconnection and disintegration, and Schönberg's 'emancipation of the dissonance' in which he establishes the equality of all twelve tones" are perhaps the most fascinating periods, and of Beethoven's last style "one could say that he reached a philosophy of discomfort." Obviously, the synthesis of "old" and "new" which Beethoven reached in his last quartets and piano sonatas, where a profound harmony and transcendent beauty is reached and realized, healing the "scars" of struggle and fragmentation, has escaped Barenboim's attention. Similarly, to suggest that these two utterly different composers operate, as it were on the same plane, is absurd, as the idea that Beethoven moved to "disconnection and disintegration," to a "philosophy of discomfort," shows the destructive influence of modernist thinking, Schönbergianizing Beethoven and Beethovianizing Schönberg, as if there were a direct line between them. And that "Schönberg is well on his way to becoming one of the most accepted twentieth century composers," as Barenboim states with unscrupulous optimism in the above-mentioned concert program, is just an embarrassing statement. Beethoven's achievement is a culmination of humanistic idealism embodied in an oeuvre that *also*, in purely artistic terms, belongs to the best the human mind has ever been able to create; also his late works are harmonious through and through, creating a new synthesis out of the contrasting elements of order and disruption, a dichotomy that was at the heart of Beethoven's creative project from the start, finding ever new combinations and solutions. Schönberg however, living in a time of disasters and a dying culture, failed to create a comparable message in his music—how could it be otherwise? He showed the devastation of the human soul in a terrifying world and his quasi-constructive answer, the twelve-tone-system, was a forced defense mechanism amidst the debris. To compare him with Beethoven, who built up a musical edifice of a spiritualized Enlightenment humanism, is denying the profound tragedy of the twentieth century when this edifice, as a symbol of European culture, had dissolved (and wept over by Mahler), a catastrophe Schönberg had to witness with a bleeding heart. And of course, he did not "establish the equality of all twelve notes" (as Barenboim's totalitarian rhetoric asserts) because in art music, there is no central authority, like a Soviet Ministry of Culture, who decides for everybody how music should be written, and certainly Schönberg's oeuvre demonstrates that music without tonality cannot exist *as music*.

Musical modernism in the last century often traces its origins back to Beethoven as the icon of progressiveness, the first genius of the modern project. But this is based upon a grave misunderstanding of Beethoven's music. There is no evidence that he thought about himself as a "modern artist" in the modern sense. Yes, he broke many molds of eighteenth-century classicism, but only to restore them on a much bigger scale. Yes, he did many courageous, new things, but not with the intention of being "modern" but to do something "better" than before, his own earlier works included. Yes, he occasionally used shockingly sharp dissonances, but his overall style is much less chromatic than Mozart's, he used his sharp dissonances as *exceptional* effects. While exploring hitherto unknown possibilities of expressing subjective emotional life experiences, he kept an attentive eye on the past, be it baroque or medieval music, or the principles or concepts of Antiquity, or Enlightenment values from the eighteenth-century philosophers. In the diary Beethoven wrote in the period 1812–1818, he mused, "If only one wanted to separate oneself from the past, still the past has created the present" (cited in Maynard Solomon's *Beethoven Essays*, Cambridge Mass., 1988, Harvard University Press).

We will see that this mentality, which combines looking back with being utterly personal and original, has its roots in Italian Renaissance thinking. The past can be an example for development without the need of being "modern" in a historical sense, as if the artist were walking on a time line into the future. Beethoven's orientation upon Antiquity is well documented, especially in the context of the "late period" in which the *9th Symphony*, the *Missa Solemnis*, and the famous *Last Quartets* were composed. As Maynard Solomon explains in the prologue of his *Late Beethoven, Music, Thought, Imagination* (University of California Press, 2003):

> One may also find in the fragmentary aesthetic pronouncements and comments that are sprinkled throughout Beethoven's letters and conversation books a rough tapestry of neoclassical, classical, and romantic ideas that increasingly highlight his participation in romantic expressive theories and his deep identification with such central concepts of Romanticism as the infinite, yearning, nostalgia, and inwardness. The tension between Beethoven's Classicist and Romanticist tendencies can be viewed as beginning a detachment from an Olympian, Winckelmannian conception of Classicism, in place of which Beethoven, in the major works of his "heroic" style, constructed a restless Classicism now imbued with a broad range of extreme images centering on death, struggle, memorialization, elegy, and festal celebration. In his music Beethoven implied — perhaps even argued — the necessity of restoring to Classicism the fusion of Apollonian decorum and Dionysian violence that Schiller and Friedrich Schlegel had shown to have been thoroughly commingled in the ancient world, a fusion to which Nietzsche — in good part via his reading of Beethoven's Ninth Symphony — was to give its lapidary expression later in the nineteenth century.

Later on, Solomon proposes that Beethoven was deeply involved in a quest to preserve essential qualities of the ancient world and that his ideal of a renovated Classicism is itself a typical characteristic of nineteenth-century Romanticism. It could therefore be argued that this endeavor may qualify Beethoven as "a representative of a Renaissance impulse in music." Solomon mentions as an example the Seventh Symphony, where the use of musical analogues of classical poetic rhythms and meters can be considered as a sign of Beethoven's participation in the Classic-Romantic revalidation of the cultural, ethical, and aesthetic premises of Antiquity. To see Beethoven as the originator of the project of musical modernism is to entirely leave out the enormous influence of the past, and notions of Antiquity, upon Beethoven's creative motivation. There is no direct line of development from Beethoven (i.e., Viennese Classicism) to Schönberg other than a merely historic succession of random events, as there may be between the architect building a house, different generations of people living in it for a period, and the construction worker who demolishes it much later. In spite of Schönberg's professions of respect for and dedication to the Viennese tradition, which he vainly tried to combine with his dodecaphonic sonic art, he may have understood something of the structuralism of that glorious period but obviously not the spirit itself which informed that structuralism.

In spite of the obvious conclusion that Schönberg's dodecaphonic experiments invites—that music without tonality cannot exist as music— something else emerged: Webern's miniature twelve-tone works which were completely overlooked during his lifetime but formed the gospel of post–Second World War serialism, giving birth to a form of art without reference to music, a new way of organizing sound which was claimed to be the normal further stage of development of Western art music. The contradiction that this sound art was supposed to be, on one hand, the result of a total break with tradition, and on the other, the result of its development, was overlooked as, in the heat of the discussions pro and contra in the 1950s and 1960s, the new art form had to establish itself against the resistance of the central performance culture and long-established notions of what music—art music—really is. According to the advocates of "new music," of which Stokhausen and Boulez were the most articulate, music had to begin all over again with the "Stunde null"—"the hour zero"—and "really relevant composers" should start from scratch and create a new field of musical experience from which notions of "expression" and "communication" were deleted as being "romantic" and "decadent" relics from the nineteenth century and thus from the civilization that gave birth to two world wars, fascism, and communism. What exactly made the work of Webern so attractive that it was "saved" from a prewar, decadent period but no other composers? The answer is simple: in contrast to what was thought to be Webern's intentions, other composers from that time still wanted to *say* something through their work, albeit sometimes willy-nilly like Stravinsky (most of his career), and therefore could not do without tonality. The irony was, of course, that in Webern's work—including the late works—the textures were still intended to be *musically* expressive, however microscopically and ineffectively, a last miniature vestige of human emotion like tiny, secret tears evaporating on the hard surfaces of acoustical diamonds: an utterly final point, a limit reached, a farewell, and an absolute defeat and end of the late-Schönbergian line of thought. Of course this "romantic" element was not noticed because that would require an alert *musical* and *psychological* sensitivity which was the last thing pursued in the post-1945 years when the *brave new world* was born. Thus, a misunderstood Webern became the martyr saint of modernism and a yardstick of progressiveness, even luring old Stravinsky in its promise of modernity when he had written out his neoclassical period and did not know what to do next.

An amusing example of the absurdity and lack of understanding of the nature of art music in this mental world of twelve-tone composition is

offered in one of the lectures Webern gave in 1932 in Vienna (later published by Universal Edition under the title *Der Weg zur Neuen Musik*). To
metaphorically demonstrate the equality of the different forms of the
series in twelve-tone composition, thus creating a thorough coherence,
Webern quotes an old Latin palindrome, a "magical square," where the
letters read in every direction—left to right, right to left, top to bottom,
bottom to top, and in the inversions—give the same message:

S A T O R
A R E P O
T E N E T
O P E R A
R O T A S

The translation of the saying, *Sator Arepo tenet opera rotas*, whereby Arepo
is the name of a person, is translated as, "The sower Arepo keeps the
work running" or "The sower Arepo holds the wheels of work." Indeed,
the square is an ingenious structure in symmetries, in which reading
from any direction produces the same result. One could imagine why
Schönberg was fascinated by the possibility of a musical structure in
which the identity of the material remained the same, whatever procedures it was subject to, because if tonality as a structural factor were
eliminated, this kind of atomic through-structuring could, maybe, still
enable a way of creating unity in the cloud of splintered tone fragments.
However, a word-play like the "magic square" is a very different matter
from composing music, and it is not without significance that the communication of the square, what it actually *says*, is a message that would
be interesting or helpful to a very limited number of people. A unifying
structure in itself is no guarantee for a meaningful communication, be it
in terms of language or music. The nonsensical results of this mental
framework show that the arithmetic obsession with "order" in this way
never had anything to do with a *musical* order, which does not need such
kind of structuring, as so many great works of the repertoire show, and
that the understanding of musical meaning had disappeared. If anything,
the "magical square" shows that the more thoroughly and regularly a
structure is organized on the material level, the less differentiation in
terms of meaning it can produce. All this was driven by the need to find a
deeper ordering, Webern explains, to be able to say in a totally new way
what had been said in former times. From this, it can be concluded that
Webern had not the faintest idea *what* it was that had been said in former
times: the difference with the past was, of course, that structure had been
closely connected with *musical* meaning made possible through tonality,
which cannot be simply translated in purely rational, mathematical relationships between separate tones. The "thorough" ordering of sound,
which seemed necessary when the expressive and structural possibilities

of tonality seemed to have "broken down," was an attempt to restore order in a way different from tonality. While *musical* ordering through tonality can create a strong coherence that leaves ample space for freedom and caprice, purely *sonic* ordering (of which Schönberg's twelve-tone-system was the first attempt) could not be related to order which has a *musical* meaning because it bypassed all the possibilities of relationships that tonality offers, and, with it, the possibility for the listener to use his hardwired receptive system: ears, brain, and heart, to experience what is going on in a piece of music. It is interesting to compare this new, materialistic attitude toward "order" with Beethoven's, the creator of phenomenally through-structured and (of course) utterly tonal works. In a conversation with musician friends, where the notion of structure was discussed, Beethoven corrected the idea that an ordering as strict as possible would be the best way of creating coherence: "Well, there must also be room for free fantasy." His music offers an instructive example of the relationship between order and freedom, where structure and free fantasy find a happy balance.

The idea of "free fantasy" derives, of course, from the tradition of free improvisation, which was a normal capacity of composers at the time and which was closely bound up with the notion of expression. Hence the freedom of structure in, to name some examples, the masterly *Eroica Symphony*, *Violin Concerto*, and *Fourth* and *Fifth Piano Concertos* which are perfectly formed but in which also a euphoric freedom reigns. It is exactly this sometimes almost wild freedom in combination with order and harmony which produces the psychologically uplifting effect of these masterpieces: if one could live like that, one would be happy for ever. The relative freedom which Boulez introduced following the strictest serialism in the 1950s, however, did not make the slightest difference between "order" and "chaos," because the result of either procedure was always the same amorphous, meaningless collection of disconnected notes and sounds. The embarrassing discovery in the 1960s that a totally structured serialism sounded, in effect, the same as a totally indeterminate work, where the sounds were the result of "free atonal improvisation" or "chance operations," underlines the obvious tenet that structure in itself has no meaning, and that in an atonal sonic sound world *any* structural principle can be used or not used, without any consequence as far as meaning is concerned. In sonic art, structure is considered in the same way as in science: it is just the way things are ordered, or not ordered, on a material level, without any relation to the notion of meaning *for humans* as far as the thing itself is concerned: does a bacteria have meaning, or iron crystals, or the orbit of Saturn? It just *is*: as the world without the human mind is, *objectively* so. Establishing a meaningful relationship through *functionality* is quite a different matter. In that case, a human need is projected upon the object to be *used*, but this has nothing to do with meaning concerning the object itself: bacteria can be used for medical purposes, iron crystals for industrial purposes, and Saturn's orbit can be scientifically researched. Pure knowledge of the objective world, of objective reality, has no meaning for the human mind in the sense that art, and art music, have meaning. A work of art is the creation by a human being for other human beings: the maker, the work itself, and the human being at the receiving end all belong to the same system of signals and communication and hence, of meaning. The material side of this system is only instrumental to meaning but not part of it—it is a means to an end and not an end in itself. Understanding the means is thus something different from understanding the end, it is the difference between the understanding of the gynecologist and of the lover.

All this "objectification" of music seemed to fit well in the postwar cultural climate, which was drenched in nihilism about civilization and full of confidence in technology and scientific progress, in which also music would have to take part, focusing upon a utopian future and breaking with a past culture in which the perception of the world was supposed to have been contaminated with subjective, mental projections and the vain search for the meaning of human life. The rhetoric of the 1950s and 1960s made musical modernism also seem like a protesting gesture against the so-called worst product of this past culture: fascism and all its crimes. Hitler loved Wagner and Bruckner, so tonality and triads became suspect (vegetarianism, another hobby horse of Hitler, was not compromised though, as his love of dogs was not). It is therefore ironic to discover that the arch fathers of modernism actually showed quite a totalitarian mentality themselves, like Schönberg's notorious assertion in the early twenties that he had discovered a system which, as he put it, would guarantee German hegemony in music for the next hundred years.

As can be read in Karen Painter's thorough study: *Symphonic Aspirations, German Music and Politics 1900–1945*, to see art music as imbued with political messages was, for both musicians and composers, normal in that period of politization of all strata of society. Webern sympathized with the Nazi ideology at a time when it was already quite obvious in which direction the new regime in Germany was heading, assuming that his music would undoubtedly be the *perfect* music for the Third Reich and being really surprised when his music fell upon the government's deaf ears since the Nazi leaders had decided that Beethoven and Wagner were much better composers to demonstrate German cultural superiority. But Webern's expectations are fully understandable: it is not difficult to see a link, in terms of mentality, between the totalitarian nature of the dodecaphonic system and fascist ideas of equality, militarism, and top-down discipline. Also, some musical intellectuals, including some of Jewish background, initially felt great sympathy for the "new Germany." In a review in 1934, a year after Hitler's spectacular coup, Theodor Adorno—whose influential *Philosophy of New Music* provided the musico-political ammunition after 1950 to support the claims of atonal modernism — invoked Joseph Goebbels in his (Adorno's) recommendation of some choral publications, obviously in sympathy with a regime that had already shown its teeth. Here, there is not much difference with the naive and misconceived optimism of Richard Strauss and Paul Hindemith who both believed that the new Germany would make necessary reforms in music life possible. Heinrich Strobel, post-1945 music director of a German radio station and the Donaueschingen Festival, another important advocate of modernism who has done a lot for the postwar Darmstadt avant-garde, recommended Goebbels' "steel-like romanticism" when reporting on the German Composers Festival in 1933, shortly after assuming the editorship of the new music journal, *Melos*. This happened after the former editor was ousted for "political unreliability." (Strobel even remained editor after the journal was Nazified and renamed *Neues Musikblatt*.) Ironically, both Adorno and Strobel sympathized with a political climate that forced them both into emigration (Adorno, and Strobel's wife, were Jewish).

In Toby Thacker's *Music after Hitler, 1945–1955*, we read that the composers Wolfgang Fortner and Hermann Heiss, who were involved in the setting up of the Darmstadt Summer School after the war, were both blacklisted by the American occupation army. Heiss had happily collaborated with the Nazi regime by writing marches, as Fortner had specialized in "festive music" for the Hitler Jugend and had conducted the Hitler Jugend Orchestra in Heidelberg. The transition from totalitarian state service to modernist musical paradigms obviously was not a very difficult one. As Thacker describes:

> Heiss was the first in post-war Germany to write extensively about twelve-tone music. At Darmstadt in 1946, he declared: "We have today a unique opportunity, with our experience and knowledge, to preserve young people from wrong turnings and detours." [. . .] Fortner also turned rapidly to twelve-tone music. Alongside Heiss and Fortner, many of the composers whose music was played at Darmstadt in 1946 were compromised, such as Degen, Pepping, Distler, and Höffer. The piano class was taken in 1946 and 1947 by former NSDAP member Udo Dammert, who was certainly persona non grata with the Americans, having falsified his "Fragebogen" (questionnaire).

The Darmstadt Summer Course, which became the ideological center of modernism in the postwar years, was set up as a symbol of cultural freedom and, as such, it was treated as propaganda, as is shown by the involvement of the American military government and Radio Frankfurt. Also, the postwar continuation of the festival of Donaueschingen, which under the Nazis had been turned into a celebration of Germanic festive and folk music, was supposed to be a sign of a return to normality in a free world, although its first postwar director, the composer Hugo Herrmann, had in earlier years conducted the National Socialist Symphony Orchestra there, in a brown dinner jacket. "The German composers whose works were played, von Knorr, Gerster, Degen, Hermann himself, were all compromised" (Thacker). In 1950, a new format of the festival corrected this all-too-easy change from one context to another and became more "acceptable," quickly developing into an international showcase for atonal modernism, which had been condemned by the Nazis as *entartet* (corrupted) and imbued with "Jewish influence."

Only from this postwar perspective can it be understood how the greatness of premodern music could be seen as stained with the curse of crime and catastrophe. The classical tradition, as it had been hijacked by absurd ideologies of "Aryan supremacy," and of which Richard Strauss was—in spite of his conflicts with the regime—the still living symbol, could not be "cancelled" as it formed the basis of the central performance culture, also in the allied nations of the West. But cutting it off from the development of new music would "free" new creation from this association and give contemporary music the aura of symbolizing the new, free world, liberated from insanity. That the modernist ideology was, in spite of the rejection of the Nazi regime, on a deeper level strongly related to the fascist mentality, as is shown by its roots in the "supremacy" cult of the Schönberg circle, the mentality of modernist "composers" with their intolerant utopian orthodoxies, and the compromised "midwives" of the first post-1945 modernist centers, makes the moral condemnations that landed on old Strauss' head after the war from the modernist camp sound pretty hypocritical, and the anti-fascist rhetoric of the avant-garde absurd, in the light of Boulez's "Napoleonic" mentality and Stokhausen's megalomania. The mental climate in modern-music life of the 1950s and 1960s showed, with their fanatic ideological quarrels, quasi party-line directives, excommunications, betrayals, and the like, the very same abject behavior that characterized totalitarian music politics. Thus, in Western Europe, a mirror image emerged of the totalitarian culture politics as practiced in the Soviet Union, with the difference that, in the free West, no government was forcing composers to write in this or that style—with the help of modernist ideologies, the composers could be trusted to organize themselves independently in such way. As of no other postwar "composer," particularly the writings of Boulez reflect the totalitarian, antihumanist mentality that can easily be related to both fascism and communism. A couple of well-known quotes will sufficiently characterize the sort of texts which were addressed to the new music scene, but inevitably leaked out into the wider world:

> "It is not enough to deface the Mona Lisa because that does not kill the Mona Lisa. All the art of the past must be destroyed."
> "Any composer who has not felt—I do not say understand—but felt the necessity of the dodecaphonic language, is USELESS."

"I think that music must be hysteria and collective spells, violently of the present."

"History as it is made by great composers is not a history of conservation but of destruction—even while cherishing what is being destroyed."

All this sounds much less innocent than Schönberg's soup tureen. According to Joan Peyser's biography of Boulez, the literary socialite Suzanne Tézenas, companion of the ardent fascist Pierre Drieu La Rochelle (who committed suicide shortly before the end of the war), was an early admirer and supporter of this upcoming modernist composer, greeting him as her new artist savior. Typically, she was not much interested in Boulez's work as such but seemed fascinated by what he represented. It is therefore no surprise to find that Boulez seems to have welcomed the infusions of German culture by the Nazis during the French occupation, as he was quoted as saying, with the air of a cultural expert: "The Germans virtually brought high culture to France"—as if France had been something like a developing country.

Condemning the past in order to begin with a clean slate, which Boulez tried to do sonically with his works of the 1950s (which attempted to celebrate violence) and with his writings (which try to shoot down everything which could be related to the high culture of the past) could hardly count as a creative beginning in terms of art. However, considering the overall nature of these writings, the modernist underlying motive becomes clear: burning down the "Alexandrine library" of musical culture, like the opera houses Boulez advocated (in the 1950s) to burn down, would remove the possibility of comparison, liberate new music from an artistic quality framework, reduce music to a one-sided, totalitarian approach (thus removing character, interpretation, and expression), streamlining a characteristic and pluralistic art form to the same neutrality and quasi-objectivity as the glass-and-steel office blocks of postwar urban landscapes.

The same mentality of aggression and destruction can already be found in the famous but absurd manifestos which accompanied the birth of nonfigurative visual art. The *Futuristic Manifesto* (1909) advocated war as the only possible hygienic treatment of the world. The *Dadaistic Manifesto* (1917) incites to mass murder, while, according to the *Second Surrealistic Manifesto* (1929), the ultimate surrealistic deed is to go into the street with a revolver and randomly shoot at people. And these trends were presented as progressiveness, as passing a threshold in the history of mankind, leaving the entire past with the unfolding of civilization of millennia behind and creating nothing less than a new world for a liberated humanity, liberated from civilization. Sometimes one stumbles upon the suggestion that progressiveness in the arts is exclusively related to Enlightenment humanism. But history tells another story. Fascism and

communism were, in the first half of the last century, generally considered "modern" and "progressive." In Russia and—after the Second
World War—Eastern Europe, twentieth-century "modernization" of society was imposed top down by the communist regimes, suppressing local
traditions which bubbled up again after the fall of the Soviet Union. And
what was considered the cradle of modernist mentality in music: Wagnerism, which the composer liked to relate to politics, became in the late
nineteenth century a broad cultural movement in Middle Europe, characterized by rightwing aggressive nationalism, antisemitism, xenophobia,
and fanatic militarism: a murky mix of antihumanistic primitivism, while
the so-called "conservative" Brahms identified himself with the enlightened *Bildungsbürgertum* of the liberal and educated bourgeoisie, of which
the art-loving Jewish upper-class community formed an important part.
It is not difficult to see which side supported civilization best.

A form of music which is not organized on the basis of the "gravity
force" of tonality is not music at all, but something else. It is indeed
nothing less and nothing more than "sound art" or "sonic art," an art
form typical of the last century and which does without the entire range
of communication and expression that had been the normal territory of
art music for ages. Sonic art has to be judged according to its own intentions and not be compared to music, which distorts both the nature of
music and of sonic art. Sonic art emerged and developed on its own
accord like photography emerged, next to painting, in the nineteenth
century; also then there was a discussion about the role of painting that
was now more or less freed from an "obligation" to represent reality in a
realistic way. At the time, painters feared that their art would become
irrelevant and superfluous—but instead photography created the possibility of impressionism, the triumph of which was possible because
"creating real pictures of the world" could now be left to photography
and painting was now free to do what photography could not do—painting could *say* things, and could *show* things that photography could not.
Painting returned from a dry realist academicism (which was a narrow-
minded nineteeth-century interpretation of tradition) to its original intention, which is a *subjective* interpretation of reality (i.e., reality as experienced through the senses and the emotions). Although academic painting
was mimetic, it could not stand comparison with the artistic qualities of
its upcoming rivals naturalism (which depicted real-life scenes in a realistic, but subjective way) and impressionism (which expressed the effects
of reality as experienced by the senses).

In the current argument, sonic art is shown to be the very art of musical modernism, the art form which reflects in an excellent and unintentionally articulate way the absence and degradation of inner life in the
modern world, the alienation of the individual, the loss of values and the
fragmentation of civilization, the erosion of transcendence, aspiration,
idealism, spirituality, beauty, sensitivity—in short, exactly those faculties

which form the higher levels of civilization and human development, the levels which can give meaning to human existence and raise us above the trivialities of physical existence. By advertising sonic art as *the* "music" that best represents modernity, composers in the 1950s and 1960s unintentionally hit the nail on its head — their only mistakes were to call their work *music* and to think that representing the *zeitgeist* was a good thing. This does not mean that sonic art has no qualities, but that its qualities are strongly bound up with the problems of the period, and it will only survive as a curious historical footnote if it has no qualities that are capable of relating to more universal human values, which can also be understood in terms of our understanding, as far as we can know, of art from the Middle Ages.

Sonic art certainly is an art form, only not a *musical* art form. This realization is, in fact, quite common among musicians who have been educated in the art of music and sometimes partake in sonic performance, for instance in an orchestral work by Xenakis, who asks from the players things which are not an extension of their craft but a negation of it: in music, performing techniques are not merely functional, physical applications to get the right sound, but are directly and organically related to the expressive values and norms of the culture and tradition of which it forms a part. In musical performance, all technique is part of the aim of expression of whatever kind, so performance technique of sonic art displays all the characteristics of the art form itself, of which the absence of *musical* imagination is the most noticeable. This, however, does not mean that a sonic performance, as performance, has no qualities in itself. The work of someone like Boulez *as music* is meaningless nonsense; but *as sonic art* it often creates a sophisticated and decorative listening experience. Alas, much sonic art (including the Boulezbian variety) loses itself in gratuitous pattern making, as if meant to avoid any possibility of irritation, like certain types of abstract painting which sometimes adorn the more expensive hotel lobbies, intended to create an up-to-date, but inoffensive, atmosphere for the guests. In comparison to a past golden age of strongly expressive masterpieces, it is no surprise that even the "best" sonic art is not of much interest to people who love *music*. The claim that sonic art is music can be understood as the main cause of the general indifference toward any new music and the irrelevance of new music in the wider context of contemporary culture; "if *this* is new music," musically sophisticated audiences think, "then music as an art form has died." And they are right.

The understanding of the difference between sonic art and music is a truth that dare not speak its name, anxious to offend the "new music establishment" which rests mainly upon myth making instead of upon powerful, musical works. Many performing musicians working in specialized "modern music ensembles" have no difficulty with this difference because they lack the qualities which would make them eligible for playing *music*. In fact, sonic art provides an appropriate working field for people, gifted in technically handling musical instruments but otherwise lacking in fundamental musicality, which always includes a sophisticated psychological sensitivity as expressed through the unfolding of musical narrative and an awareness of the inner life in which this narrative takes place. It is therefore no surprise that we find among them often a materialistic, functionalistic mentality comparable to the "idealism" which created the glass-and-steel architecture that adds such a disastrous contemporary comment to the fabric of Europe's historic cities. It is not that sound art players have no abilities, as specialist ensembles like the French *Ensemble Intercontemporain* and the German *Ensemble Modern* attest; only, their sophistication is not a *musical* one since music is not expected from them. Boulez's own recording of his *Marteau sans Maitre* of 2005 for DGG with the *Ensemble Intercontemporain* is ample proof of the enormous investment of precision and acoustical sophistication in a result that goes no further than a pointillist collection of refined surface effects without any musical meaning. Also Boulez's so-called "masterpiece" *Répons*, another example of sonic investment, is a work with a busy surface and cool, decorative sonorities, which here and there include snippets of chords from the musical field, but disconnected and absorbed in an acoustical field without an interrelated network of tonal connections, and thus static, meaningless, "objective," like the style of *La Défense*, Paris, a pathetic, modernist imitation of New York. This cubist quarter which spoils the sky line of the elegant Champs Elysées boulevard, represents the attempt to bring Paris, one of the most beautiful and poetic of European cities, "up to date"—as a belated gesture of sympathy to the notorious modernist architect Le Corbusier who proposed, in the 1950s, to replace Paris' city center with square modernist tower blocks. From these destructive misconceptions the "modern world" was born, a world of glass and steel, of flat, glimmering surfaces, of smooth bureaucracy, control, collectivist and corporate power, and abstract order. Sonic art is the best acoustical reflection of this *brave new world* and as it is relatively easy to design buildings purely on the basis of function and new mass-produced materials, and without the difficult philosophical questions of style, expression, artistic meaning, cultural representation, and relation to tradition and to architectural and natural environments, it is for quite some people a relief to be able to pursue the career of a "composer" without all the weight and problems of musical craftsmanship, personality, historic awareness, psychological and aesthetic sensibility that music, as a form of high art, requires. But as a form of playful acoustic entertainment or decoration, sonic art is harmless and can occasionally attain an interesting beauty, as, for instance, in Morton Feldman's *Coptic Light* for orchestra, which is a sophisticated tapestry of slowly changing sound colors, so much more interesting than Boulez's flickering "flea music" or Stokhausen's acoustical pretensions. Also the sonic art of, for example,

Georg Friedrich Haas often achieves an effect of surface beauty, where he makes use of friendly, consonant intervals while avoiding the possibilities of narrative and the development of inner space. The best this art can achieve is a meditative atmosphere, or a morbid and oppressing one like the work of Pascal Dusapin, whose morbid soundscapes evoke the climate of nightmares, which can in itself be something of interest. This kind of sonic art is like a shadowy, ghostly reflection of far-away music, random and decorative, like the anxious look of someone locked up in darkness but with a small window through which a sunlit square can be seen—a square surrounded by classical buildings. It is the materialistic approach toward sound by its artists which hinders sonic art, even its best pieces, from becoming music. Its most sophisticated handling of the sound surface cannot hide the psychological emptiness that makes this art so ephemeral. Nonetheless, if not considered as music, the better sonic art should be respected and maybe even enjoyed. But it should be left to art music to provide—like every serious art form—a metaphorical image of interior experience, to express the inner life of man, including the ideal, the aspirational, and the transcendent, whereby the sonic aspect of music is a means to an end and not an end in itself.

Now the question arises of how tonality as a tool of art music is related to the experience of communication and expression. Let us first turn to sonic art: can't it also be expressive? Obviously, dependent upon the context, sonic art *can* have an expressive effect upon many listeners, however hard sonic artists try to present their work as objective sound; it creates experiences of alienation and chaos for the listener who tries to listen to it *as music*, because there is no tonal focus point to which the notes relate, as it titillates the ear of the listener who listens to it as to decorative variations in acoustical "events" (i.e., a listening in purely materialistic terms for which such a tonal focal point is not necessary). It goes without saying that listeners who hardly have experience with listening to and understanding music have the least difficulty with listening to sonic art, which does not say, or express, things, but merely presents itself as a collection of acoustical events. It is not expressive as music is expressive because there is a fundamental difference between an object as such and an art form. A garbage bin or an unmade bed do not *express* things but may *represent* something, and it is in this category that the "expressiveness" of sonic art should be understood: sound as such is different from music because music transforms sound into emotional, psychical expression, it goes far beyond its physical presence, while sonic art stops there. This difference goes down to the heart of the concept of musicality itself: musicality is the capacity to understand what a musical work does, which is creating a mental space in which the musical energies move in forms, narratives, and flows, and which can be emotionally experienced by both the performing musician and the listener. To paraphrase Roger Scruton in his *Understanding Music*, the understanding of music consists of listening with the imagination, hearing *in* the sounds of the work the interior space that it creates. This can be compared with the way we look *into* the imaginary space in a painting suggested by the perspective created by the painter. Such a way of looking, and of hearing, is an imaginative action of the mind which is "programmed" to "finish" suggested patterns which are almost automatically interpreted as "complete," as a "Gestalt." The musical space is defined by harmonic backgrounds, against which the foreground figuration of melodic lines and rhythm form the surface. Patterns made up of melodic or rhythmic cells move through key areas, ordering the different elements of design and often enriched with sound color. All these defining elements together form the "bedding" through which the musical energies flow, forming a narrative unfolding in time. The force that holds the interplay of energies together is, as we have seen above, the "aural perspective" of tonality to which all parameters of melodic line, harmony, meter, and rhythm are related. This integrated design of musical space is in its dimensions much like physical space in the natural world. In listening to music, the inner self of the listener (the "I") can experience the space of the work, in his imagination he can "enter" it as he can enter a three-dimensional physical space, and "live through" the movement of the energies, which together form the piece. Or, one could say that the piece "enters" the interior space of the listener and has him experience the energetic flows that happen within the music.

The most striking characteristic of a (good) musical work is that the interplay of these energies produces effects that closely resemble those of emotional processes, or emotional processes accompanying conscious, intellectual processes, so that in the listening process the listener can identify his own emotional range with that of the musical work. It is a relationship that can be called a resonance, and it is this resonance that forms the "bridge," as it were, of communication and expression that is fundamental to musical culture. It is in this relationship that musical meaning emerges: the ordering and stylization of emotional experiences, the creation of depth and unity where otherwise fragmentation reigns, or the disclosure of hitherto unknown emotional capacities. It is a form of internally active participation, or identification, on the part of the listener, even if he sits still and silent. In his admirable book *Music and the Mind* (1992), Anthony Storr writes about this process of identification:

> Psychoanalysts refer to this participation as "projective identification": the process by which a person imagines himself to be inside some object external to himself. Imitation is not only the sincerest form of flattery, but a way of learning. By identifying ourselves with those more gifted, we can actually improve our own capacities. Teachers of music know that "do it the way I do" is often a more effective way of teaching than theoretical instruction.

This identification can also happen between a musical work and the listener. Music—that is, serious, classical, tonal music—often has a positive influence upon the inner life of the listener, because it orders emotional energies. But this participation is only possible through tonality, which is the tool that makes this resonance between the interior world of the listener (i.e., his or her musical receptivity) and the musical work possible: these two worlds are based upon the same natural ordering of sound, and it cannot be replaced by other tools, at least not with the same effect and result. Our perceptive capacities for tonality are hardwired in our brain, and only through the resonance created by tonality is it possible for the listener to perceive the shifting networks of relations between the tones as a "virtual space" that can be aurally and emotionally experienced: the space in which the interplay of the tonal energies forms patterns of changing intensity and coloring. The listener does not need to know *how* this process works; if sensitive enough, he can *experience* it, as if he were in the middle of it; whatever form or structure informs the music is subliminally noticed and makes the effect of the music in the listener possible. This is why listeners often have the feeling that the music "speaks" to them about themselves, in an orderly way, as if it were a person with an intimate knowledge of the listeners' inner life with which it resonates.

The remarkable thing is that while the musical work expresses emotional processes, it does this as an autonomous structure with its own musical logic; it can only emotionally communicate something if it is coherent and logical in terms of "pure" music—i.e., a logic along purely musical lines and not determined by factors outside the musical work (the challenge of writing songs and operas lies in the requirement of *both* following the narrative logic of a text and the logic of purely musical energies). This ambiguity has been the cause of much brain-wringing philosophical burrowing, because music does not "say" things in the way language says things, and musical logic is something fundamentally different from linguistical logic. In a logical and stylized way, and in the hands of the gifted composer, music *forms* and *invokes* emotional processes in itself, in the performer, and in the listener. It is the holistic art form *par excellence*. In comparison, sonic art is "flat," it has no inner space because the perspective and the binding force of tonality is lacking, and thus it is incapable of expressing something like "inner life." Even where performance conditions of a sonic work are prescribed, which place the players at different locations in the concert hall, the 3D effect is purely physical and not musical. A wider distribution of sound beyond the podium can only be random if there is no tonal, inner space.

The notion that music can create its own "virtual" space in which energies move, energies that can be experienced as such and which can create strong emotional responses (while in a *material* sense there is nothing that "moves" or that addresses itself directly to the listener) gives music the aura of a mystical or metaphysical presence. Indeed—the very thing thing defines music is immaterial because it is not the *sound* of the tones that create the inner space, but their *relationships*. This relates music to language and emotions, which are also in themselves immaterial and products of the human spirit. In old-fashioned terms: music is the language of the soul expressed through the network of relationships of different tones, it is the expression of the human condition. That this is possible at all is something miraculous, and it is understandable that such a thing only meets skeptical treatment by people who either have no sense of the musical, or have reasons to deny music's "virtual" space because it reminds them of the entire apparatus of religion, metaphysics, "spiritual hocus pocus," and all the "nonsense of superstition," the entire dimension of human thought and feeling in which they cannot believe.

Good, real music can capture fleeting emotional sensations that we otherwise can merely recapture by recollection, which is in itself a powerful instrument of understanding oneself and the world, as the French author Marcel Proust's incomparable exploration of memory and meaning shows (the celebrated multi-tome novel *A la Recherche du Temps Perdu*). But music can make us *experience* emotional sensations, be they new or remembered, as if the moment which provoked them is re-enacted, "extracted" from the flow of time (so to speak) and from its initial cause, placed outside the context of temporality, made timeless and thus always accessible as a direct presence in performance. One example from many possible sensations—and an explanation of the need for audiences to hear old masterpieces again and again—is the unusual atmosphere of the first movement of Beethoven's *Fourth Piano Concerto*. It can be argued that in this movement's mood of tender euphoria the emotional, conceptless essence of a real-life experience is captured, like the smell and color of a flower but without the flower itself. Imagine you are walking in a landscape which has just opened itself up to the magic of spring: you are young, full of energy, you walk with a featherlight step and feel the blood flowing through your body as to be prepared for action. But you are also strangely moved by the pure colors of unfolding nature, the silvery air you breathe, the deep blue of a bright sky, as if nature and life is born for the first time, and together with the feeling of energetic flow the heart is filled with a mixture of awe and tenderness. No shadow—neither in yourself nor in the surrounding field, which rustles with impatience, full of expectation of something utterly beautiful and spectacular, something that will surely come but which is still unknown. Most of the shades of emotion which would be part of this experience are captured in this wonderful movement so that they can be enlivened again and again, as if the listener is undergoing the very experience that may have given birth to this work, and not as a recollection (which would be rather bland in comparison) but as *real life experience*. In this way, the fleeting *essence* of life—which lies in experience and not in concepts—is made "eternal," and our love for this kind of masterpieces finds its source in the realization that our own essence, which is also nonconceptual, is confirmed by this type of experience. A fleeting emotional experience has been taken out of the context of physical reality and has been stylized into a work of art in the form of a "narrative" of musical energies, whereby its essence has been liberated from temporal ballast and thus made available and accessible to other people. All conceptual/exterior elements which throw up the differences between people, between cultures, between historical periods, have been removed and only the universal essence of inner experience has remained. This process of capturing emotional essence is the secret of the popularity of great composers like Bach, Mozart, Beethoven, Wagner, Mahler, Debussy, and so forth, and as long as people seek transcendence of their conceptual, temporal world, they will need this musical experience to feel their own humanity and the atemporal quality of their soul confirmed. Together with the experience of human love, there hardly is a stronger source of psychic energy. Indeed, the experience of masterly music is very close to the experience of real human love: in both, a spiritual factor is at work, confirming the immortality of our inner being.

It is interesting to note that the denying attitude toward these kinds of musical experiences can also be found with traumatized people, victims of war, violence, state-induced misery under dictatorships, and the like. In the winter of 2005, the German theorist and composer Wolfgang Andreas Schultz published a remarkable essay in the cultural magazine *Lettre International: Avantgarde und Trauma*, in which he showed the link between musical modernism and war trauma. Both after the First and the Second World War, collective and individual trauma gave a strong stimulus to the development of modernist thought and practice, which denied the immaterial, psychological dimension of music, which operates in the multifarious differentiations of the emotional field. Traumatized people often eschew the emotional territory altogether, because getting in touch with emotional reactions to horror is just too painful. So, as a survival mechanism, the entire emotional field is "blocked," and the intellect focuses upon rational control, in the way a drowning man clings to his lifebelt. But this reaction looks, on a surface level, the same as the characteristic swagger of over-rationalistic people with a seriously *underdeveloped* emotional life, including the faculty of emotional intelligence, so important to art and especially, music. Both types of people cling to the same type of lifebelt, but one of them is in the water, the other is on safe dry land. So, if sonic artists like Stockhausen, Boulez, and Xenakis—being young during World War II—had suffered emotional trauma and thus avoided expressive possibilities as a form of escapism from strings too sensitive to touch, their stance could be welcomed by people who were emotionally and artistically seriously underdeveloped. The trajectory from trauma through suppression and escapism toward the institutionalization of incompetence shows itself all too clearly; the exclusion of the human/all too human offered compensations, too great and too reassuring, for both the damaged human soul and the incompetent poseur, to forego. But art—real art—can only thrive if its humanity, in all its grandeur and fragility, is given space to operate. One is reminded of the touching story of a young English soldier, returning from the devastating horrors of the trenches of World War I, casually joining a couple of friends on a visit to the National Gallery and suddenly breaking down in tears in front of a Botticelli Madonna surrounded by putti; the painting brought him in touch with the feelings of innocence, tenderness, and beauty that had been locked up in the deepest dungeon of the subconscious because of experiences too destructive to feel them. This story is a good example of art as an ideal repository of human values, without which life becomes like an orchestral sonic piece by Elliot Carter, whose intention it is to "celebrate" modern life with its materialistic bustle and superficial speed. Life as a merely rationalistic and physical enterprise robs the human being of exactly the values that make him human and raise him above the animalistic sphere, the sphere that caused the twentieth-century wars in the first place. Musical modernism has aptly created the experience of this vision of life, and listeners enjoying its products *as music* are to be pitied, rather than respected as representing a "culturally advanced" elite, as was advocated by the "avant-garde" of yore.

Whatever nonphysical presence there was in modernism was merely intellectual theory and rationalistic structuring, which could not be perceived in the listening experience. The bestiality of two world wars destroyed—in many people—the belief in the possibility of a metaphysical or spiritual reality and thus it was logical to also dismiss any possible immaterial presence that music might have or represent. Modernism in all arts has long roots in the nineteenth century, and in many ways it can be considered the ultimate realization of the extreme form of romantic utopianism, mingled with reactions to and influences from the industrial revolution and increasing modernization of especially the cities. But war greatly intensified its development, more drastically than anything else. War does not only destroy human bodies, it also destroys human souls.

In recent times, in certain trends of philosophy, the idea has emerged that the "self" (i.e., the self-awareness as a unique individual with an inner life, a mind, a free will, and personal responsibility) is only a "construct," an artificial creation, a mask, to interact with other people and to function within a socially constructed environment, but not the "I" as we experience it. According to this view, our experience of identity would rest upon self-suggestion and would just be a kind of romantic fiction: we delude and flatter ourselves by imagining that the construct of self is our innermost experienced "I" but it is in reality merely a wishful projection. Also, in neuroscience sometimes an expert stands up to optimistically declare that we are just a bag of neurons and that our personality can be changed by a medication that changes the chemistry of the brain, *thus* our personality is merely the result of physical properties and nothing more. In the same superficial way, it is no unusual exception when a neuroscientist claims that we do not have a free will, because research has shown that even in the case of what we think is a rational consideration, decision, or a rational impulse of free willpower, before our rational decision there is already activity in the part of the brain which is related to purely instinctive and emotional stimuli, i.e., our experience of free will is a false one because it is directed by deeper drives of which we are not aware. That this is only the physical confirmation of the existence of what psychology calls the "subconscious," a very early and basic assumption in the history of research of the human mind and proven empirically over the last hundred years as a workable and true one, an assumption which was already put forward by Schopenhauer in the early nineteenth century and thus nothing new or spectacular, shows the problems which arise when scientists overspecialize and lack the necessary general erudition which would have given them a better perspective with which to evaluate their own research outcomes. Both the idea that the self is an artificial construct and that it is only the result of physical activities of the brain over which we have no control, can only emerge in people with a seriously underdeveloped inner life and a fundamental lack of knowledge and understanding of human nature and civilization. It is not the place here to refute these misconceptions in detail but it should be clear that these mistakes are mistakes of interpretation: if these assertions were true, it would not be possible to experience in the reality of life something like "free will" and "personal responsibility" as empirically workable assumptions which lead to concrete results; also the entire dimension of morality, ethics, and justice would become meaningless, and it would be impossible to understand classical music's profound influence upon our inner experience of self and identity. We would then also not be able to discern meaning in classical works, because it would be impossible to take a position outside the human sphere and examine the matter purely objectively. The "identity" of a Beethoven symphony could then as well be a mere social construct, meant to socially interact with our own mask and offering nothing of substance and identity underneath—in other words, we would only listen to a mask and never know the real thing, if there was any.

The observation that in our interaction with our social environment we present a certain public "face" is also an old psychological observation: it was already described by C. G. Jung as the "persona," the normal shell which protects us in human interaction and which can be dropped when we are in company that we can fully trust (i.e., when we can show our real self). In the same way do neuron firings just before we take a "free" decision not determine whether we decide something on free will or not; we are free to react this or that way upon emotional impulses, as everybody with a minimum of self-reflection can attest. The long tradition of the humanities, which is based upon experience and interpretation, provides the best instrument to deal with questions like this; if certain overzealous scientists had a thorough grounding in psychology, philosophy, and especially the philosophy of science (which would define both capacities and limitations of science), they would never come up with such limited and thus wrong conclusions, which can be quite disheartening for uninformed people who are under the illusion that science has the last word upon their reality.

The idea that "the mind" is a set of operations carried out by the brain, does not contradict the notion of the mind as an inner space of consciousness, as the observation that the sound coming from a radio set is caused by the reception and processing of radio waves does not contradict the identity and meaning of the broadcast program. The problem here is the blurring of two different levels of reality. The adoration of technical facilities by immature and uneducated minds seems to give the impression that the human mind is just like a machine, a kind of super computer. This kind of thinking reduces intelligent reflection and the capacity of discerning value and meaning, which can never be "digitalized." The negative influence of these kinds of misconception upon the meaning of high art will be clear.

It may be appropriate here to quote the young philosopher Morgan Meis in a review of a neuroscientific book on an internet site of Drexel University, Philadelphia (www.thesmartset.com):

> We are broadly aware of the fact, for instance, that there has been a vast accretion of knowledge about the natural world and about ourselves over the last two centuries. We are also broadly aware that the understanding we have gained has not been neutral. It has not left the world as it was. The understanding has transformed our relationship to the world, to one another, to ourselves. Maybe that is a simple way to describe the sense of crisis that has always been a constituent part of the experience of modernity. As we understand differently, we act differently. And how you act is, in some fundamental way, how you are. So, we have changed in who we are. We have become different. How different? No one can say, exactly. Has it been for the better or for the worse? Opinions are divided. The feelings of anxiety, though, are real and they've always been real.

It seems to be clear that giving too much authority to the achievements of modernity, in the sense of drawing from the expanded knowledge of the material world all kinds of conclusions for the human psyche which operates on so many other levels as well, leads to the erosion of the humanities, of the understanding of human inner life, which again can lead to serious misrepresentations of the very reality under examination. There is no "proven fact" in the natural world that would contradict the typical workings of human consciousness and the nature of inner experience, which in turn form the basis of civilization. When science made aspects of material reality understandable, interpretation of phenomena changed, but not human nature and its existential questions. The understanding that there is no "God" like an old man with beard and crown on a cloud, does not change the religious experience as such: the bottle may get another label but the wine remains the same. Denying the existence of the wine because the bottle has undergone an elaborate examination process is to ignore the total picture of reality, which — in the way we can experience it — includes so much more than the level of causation and physical laws. The material and natural world is the specific field of science, but the pretentions of scientists that they can, with scientific tools, enter territories where the scientific mental apparatus is hopelessly inadequate, turns science on its head and, instead of an enrichment of our understanding of the world, it becomes downright destructive. Human experience includes much more than the specific territory covered by science. And — as the last century amply showed — a civilization can develop effective technology and science and, at the same time, be utterly barbaric. Science will never be able to prevent civilization from decline.

THREE

The Fallacy of Modernism II: The Attack upon Music

The claim that sonic art is music is based upon ignorance of the existence of an entire dimension of human experience which is not in itself material—a dimension which forms an important part of our reality. It will be clear that these very restricted views of reality all come from the same dehumanizing source. In a culture where the entire dimension of the spirit is marginalized or has disappeared, the gates are opened to ideas which can only do harm and which will add to the destruction of our civilization and to the precious knowledge and understanding embodied in its high art—among which is classical music. It follows from this line of thought that the cultivation of interiority, of which music is one of its most impressive manifestations, is crucial to the survival of our civilization, and that classical music as a whole is central to the much-needed renaissance of European cultural identity on all levels (which will also have implications for the Americas).

The claim that sonic art is music has caused an immense cloud of confusion in the musical world, and has, in fact, had the effect of a frontal attack upon music as an art form. It has caused fierce rejection of sonic art by musicians and music lovers, and as fierce a condemnation of music (especially its status in the central performance culture) by sonic artists (modernist "composers") and their advocates, because the framework of these discussions, as handled by the new music establishment, was the model of historic progressiveness. The idea that criticizing sonic art as music would represent a conservative position, and would therefore be at odds with modernity, has thrown a blanket over the real question of how art music could develop in modern times. In fact, modernist "composers" of today, like Helmut Lachenmann with his death cult, Brian Ferneyhough with his *horror vacui*, and Elliott Carter with his "celebration" of modern life, are the real conservatives, as far as this kind of label has to be administered at all. The notions of "progressive" and "conservative" are meaningless in art, where artistic quality and expressive capacity is all and history irrelevant for the experience of the work of art as such. If this were not so, it would be nonsensical to look at "old" paintings or listen to Bach or read Shakespeare or Proust.

Another peculiar result of modernism, one which had an enormous impact upon modernists' self-image, should be mentioned: by deleting the entire psychological and emotional dimension from music as being inessential and a mere cultural appendage from a decadent past, the postwar avant-garde also deleted the tools with which its products could be assessed in psychological and aesthetic terms, which are—after all—the bottom line of value judgment in art. As a result, the nature of the overwhelmingly negative effects of so many modernist works upon musicians and audiences was completely missed and the audiences' negative reactions simply explained away as "conservative"—a severe case of collective *anosognosia*. After half a century of exposure to indigestible sonic art, audiences of *music* still react in the same way, though indifference has replaced the more vocal rejection of yore—you don't have to be a conservative to hear that sonic art is *not* music. It can now be concluded that the idea of the postwar avant-garde as a clear-sighted elite far ahead of a conservative audience was outright ridiculous.

What is progress? Progress is what enhances civilization and the quality of life. Although norms of what defines "civilization" change over time, humanity learns from experience and gradually develops a universal image of man which does justice to his inborn qualities and his capacities to create the kind of life, of society, in which he can flourish and develop as a human being. The deletion of the entire dimension of interior emotional experience, aesthetic sensitivity, and awareness of the achievements of past generations, which was at the heart of musical modernism, can never be progress but only decline and self-destruction.

Sonic art has developed its own collection of conventions and clichés, a "tradition" of anti-traditionalism. Begun as a kind of cultural critique and carried by the rhetoric of anti-traditionalist "heroism," it now finds a cozy home in the hands of well-adapted youngsters who know perfectly well how to conform to the requirements of the "modern circuit" mythologies, like the German sound artist Jörg Widmann, who sells his nicely polished, harmless trade to handfuls of equally adapted sonic listeners, although it cannot find much of a sympathetic ear in the concert halls of the central performance culture where it is exposed to comparisons with music. How far this is removed from a composer like György Kurtag, who returned to a form of expressionism as inspired by Schönberg and his circle, (and thus still music, albeit on the edge of what music can do). Where Schönberg predicted disaster, Kurtag evokes a postcatastrophic psychic landscape where all life has evaporated and only faint signals of what was mark the view (*Grabstein für Stephan*; *Stèle*). It is obvious that Kurtag mourns exactly those qualities of human civilization which were lost throughout the last century. Although more musical and expressive than, for instance, Wolfgang Rihm's mostly hollow neo-expressionism with its quasi-melodramatic gestures in which the location of the notes do not matter, Kurtag repeats the twentieth-century convention of cele-brating nihilism, destruction, and desolation; as an expressive and nostal-gic reflection, this music may describe the spirit of the last century quite well — but it is impossible to build a new music on these crumbled ruins. It must be said, however, that Rihm's more recent works show an in-creasing absorption of tonality and thus, a more *effective* expressiveness, as in his free-tonal *Lichtes Spiel* for violin and orchestra (2009), which demonstrates what he could do if he had not wasted his time with pre-tentious and ineffective Bergian clichés.

Sonic art concerns itself with sound as sound (i.e., as an acoustical "object," "event," or "process"), the aesthetic/artistic meaning of which is not embedded in the experience of the resulting sound itself, which is not possible because the sound objects, events, or processes are presented and contextualized as objective: they are materials that mean, before any-thing else, *themselves*. Any meaning attached to the result has to be indi-cated by the use of suggestive titles, manuals for listening, philosophical excursions and the like, and thus form no part of the work of art itself. Tones, which are isolated sounds at a certain focused pitch, as in music, do often appear in sonic art, but to avoid any association with music the tone has to be presented isolated from other tones, for the obvious reason that — according to our hardwired tonal reception system — the ear would automatically try to relate one tone to another following the laws of har-monic overtones, the natural way of making sense of separate tones with-in a context that is supposed to be ordered. So, in sonic art, much effort goes into avoiding suggestively tonal relationships, and thus, the result is mostly characterized by a fragmented sound surface consisting of isolat-ed tones, where continuity — if intended — is created by gestures, like the throwing of confetti at festive occasions, or someone trying to mime a message without speaking. This materialist and "objective" point of de-parture is a fundamental tenet of sonic art, without which it would sound like a very bad and primitive imitation of music. There is thus a wilful antimusical element built into the basis of sonic art, which keeps it strictly within the boundaries of objective, material sound.

The lack of any psychological dimension that can be experienced in the listening process thus means that sonic art entirely operates on an acoustical surface level. When we think of the concept of cliché, we know that clichés operate on the surface of things, to avoid any deeper meaning because those deeper layers would require a different and stronger effort than the easy gesture of imitation. If we take the trouble to listen to many different examples of sonic art (to name but a few examples: Jörg Widmann, Beat Furrer, Helmut Lachenmann, Karlheinz Stockhausen, Brian Ferneyhough), we are struck by the likeness of all these various efforts, and indeed—it is not difficult to arrive at the conclusion that this territory is rife with cliché, for the obvious reason of its fundamentally materialistic surface quality. Its restriction to the materialistic surface makes it, in fact, almost impossible to avoid cliché: after the first attempts at sonic art, it was very hard to avoid its easy imitation, however different the structuring. It lacked the wide dimension of psychology that opens up the possibility of different interpretations of the same material, as in music. The many borrowings of a Mozart, Beethoven, Brahms, or Mahler have been possible because of the psychological—thus immaterial—dimension of music where the authentic personality of the composer can express itself and stamp the material with his own taste and invention. So, an art form that was initially considered progressive, avant-garde, explorative, antibourgeois, antitraditional, and offering a creative alternative to the "clichés" of a supposedly worn out musical tradition, created itself something of an apotheosis of cliché, which is all the more absurd in light of its state-supported institutionalization. And if, in an attempt to break through its isolation, educational projects try to interest children in the beauty of sonic art, hoping to be able to create something of an audience and thus, the possibility of its survival in the future, the antimusical clichés are thus fed into the minds and hearts of young people who mostly have had no musical experience that would enable them to make comparisons and thus resist this sinister attempt at undermining any budding sense of the musical. Let it be clear that if these projects were presented ostentatiously as *sound art* entertainment, as separate from *music*, they could be innocent; presenting them as an introduction to *contemporary music* can only be considered as an attack upon cultural development, an attack upon the most vulnerable group: the innocent young. To protect this group—and audiences at large—from the misunderstandings and misrepresentations of the established "modern music" consensus, the difference between sonic art and music should be in the foreground of anybody's considerations about the survival of music in the modern world.

Of course, there is also "new music," combining elements from sonic art and music. The more it navigates on the gravitational field of tonality, the more it is music, and the more chance that it creates the inner space that is the precondition of the possibilities of expression. A good demonstration of what tonality does, even in an atonal environment, can be found in the decorative modernist piece *Acrostic Wordplay* by the Korean composer Unsuk Chin. The work has a brilliant, pointillist surface of colorful complexity, in which the exact placing of the notes is irrelevant because they do not form tonal relationships. But in the fifth "scene" this glittering surface envelops a major triad that suddenly binds the whole collection of notes together and adds a tonal perspective to the sound.

The random notes suddenly achieve the meaning of additional ornamentation, and a hierarchy is established and an inner space is formed. It is as if a light is thrown upon a sound mass, which otherwise would be an interesting but rambling collection of fragmented effects, and is thus anchored. The sound becomes music, which is also much helped by modal lines that are repeated with slight variations. One would wish that the composer had taken this combination of structural means as a point of departure for the idiom of the entire piece instead of as a local exception, as a kind of "quote" from another field of experience.

A comparable combination of centrifugal chaos and a touch of binding order, demonstrating the power of tonal gravity, can be heard in Berio's *Sinfonia*, which is well-known for its brilliant and pointless quotation movement, but holds a far more interesting aspect in its *first* movement, where atonal sound shattering is alternated, time and again, by a fixed diatonal chord of the seventh, thus creating a dramatic tension comparable to the tension between dissonance and consonance in music. The expressive effect is like someone hanging with his fingertips on the edge of a precipice, clinging desperately to the tonal chord while looking anxiously into the abyss. It goes without saying that this would be an apt symbolism for the psychological state of the last century as a whole.

The fashion of including quotes or fragments from music into sonic works in the late 1960s and '70s reflected a nostalgia for expression and dramatic means, which had been lost by embracing modernist ideologies. Using quotes as a *Fremdkörper*, in the way fragments from shattered works of art are held up with tweezers, it was somehow considered acceptable and has been a nostalgic or ironic "wink" toward a lost past ever since.

Another example of sound art getting closer to music is Boulez's *Derive—2* (1988/2002), in which the virtuosic and utterly nervous "flea music" is bound together in more homogenized gestures and more quasiharmonic tone combinations than many of his earlier works. The effect is like someone trying desperately to glue together a mosaic of the miniature fragments of a pulverized fresco from former times. It is rather tragic to think of someone who first wants to destroy something and then tries to glue the splinters together. Also, the later works of Elliott Carter have mellowed a bit, as can be heard in his recent "Interventions" (typical modernist title) for piano and orchestra (2007), where he melancholically harkens back to the dark world of pretentious constipation of late Schonberg . . . a blind groping for the exit from the box in which "modern music" had locked itself.

Recapitulating: sonic art, this typical fruit of the last century, is *not* music, but an independent art form; as "conceptualism" in the world of the visual arts is *not* art but something else—a demonstration of ideas with the help of objects or events, but without aesthetics and artistic craft. Sonic art has been taken much too seriously, and to judge it with the critical apparatus of music is as unfair as it is to look for artistic craft or expression in Damien Hirst's cut corpses in formaldehyde. The resistance of audiences toward sonic art as an intruding intervention in a music program is thus fully justified—it is not the reaction of conservatism, but the normal reaction to something that does not belong in the context of an art music performance. How often is the presentation of a sonic work within a normal music program not something like the appearance of a gorilla at a wedding party, or like a drunk interrupting a yoga class? (Is kicking out the drunk conservative?) It is not very difficult to understand that, from this direction, no great art can ever be expected, and the same could be said of process music which, however, is at least a form of *music*. If ever a really great composer would emerge, someone with a musical talent comparable to Bach's or Beethoven's, he would want to employ precisely all the powers and means of craftsmanship that the art form can offer, and only in the past he would find them, and inevitably they would all relate to the possibilities of tonality and thus, to the inner world of human experience. The last thing he would want to be is "modern," as formulated in the last century.

In the 1950s and 1960s, a veritable storm of heated discussion raged in magazines, reviews, foyers, and conferences about new music. Under the delusion of defending progress, advocates of "the new" fought against the forces of "the old," like the quasi-revolution of 1968. No doubt some people in positions of responsibility were justly questioned about their motives and competence, which should be normal in a Western democracy, but it is surprising to see how the generation of "revolutionaries" from the 1960s—both in politics and music life—soon occupied the plush with a conservative mentality, far exceeding that of their erstwhile opponents. In the then gradually establishing "new music scene," this brand of opinion makers combined the usual conservative self-assertion with the ideologies of modernism, even where modernism as such had eroded, petrifying their outlook with the Berlin Walls of a misplaced idealism. In the course of time they were supported by a host of music journalists and academics who discovered in the defense of sonic art a rewarding activity, opening up wide vistas of theorizing and speculation. Since sonic art operates on the material sound surface and with rationalistic philosophies, interpretation and analysis were offered a much more concrete grip than the more psychological and emotional properties of music. By writing up sonic art, theorists and journalists could feel heroic—fighting for a noble cause—plus, they had the reward of the infinite perspective of explanation.

Since sonic art is incapable of expression, of "speaking" on its own accord as music does, its intentions and its workings needed to be clarified all the time, and the "logical" development from Wagner via Schönberg and Webern to Boulez, had to be painted again and again on a canvas of history that had nothing to do with reality and everything to do with the projection of scientific notions of progress onto all the changes that happened in music history. However, it is very hard to present the rupture of atonality as a logical outcome of *musical* developments and thus, either the difference between music and sonic art had to be ignored, or music—the music of the premodernist past, especially the music of the nineteenth century, which was supposed to carry the weight of decadence and implications of war—had to be presented as something that had become meaningless to the modern mind. A revealing and broadly representative example of the last attitude can be found in a widely read informative book on new music from 1977 by the Dutch composer and theorist Ton de Leeuw (also published in English: *Music of the Twentieth Century*), which asserts in the introduction:

> As individualism is increasing, there are signs which point towards a decrease of subjectivism. Debussy, an outstanding example of individualism, had a close relationship with nature, but one that was already different from the romantics. The romantic composer projects himself into nature, Debussy—in the first place—listens. Also Webern listens. Silence becomes audible. A new world opens up. Who has the right ears, will hear the new sound. It is the sound of an overwhelming universe in which man has lost his central place. The gardens of Versailles, the idyllic Wiener Wald, give way to the mysteries of micro- and macrocosm.

Here, in one grand sweep and with short sentences, breathless with utopian excitement, a typical modernist subject—the universe (no less)—is set against the humble attempts of humanity as expressed (and this is crucial) in nicely ordered public gardens. In other words, it is as if there never had been a Bach, a Beethoven, a Wagner, or Mahler who also occasionally contemplated the mysteries of life (including the universe), but as *experienced* by human inner life and not as processes *independent* from human experience, as "objective" representations in which the human presence is irrelevant. Indeed Debussy *listens*, he *expresses* what he hears as an ultrasensitive human being, and in an art that is a summum of artistic subtlety and expression, which does not need grandiloquence to make its point. In the quote, we see in a nutshell one of the main causes behind the claims of sonic art as a kind of music: only if you fail to experience the inner space of music and its meaning can you reject the entire musical repertoire as a naive and underdeveloped way of organizing things, much like nice public gardens and as opposed to the "more sophisticated" structuring of sonic art, like the structures of macro- and microcosm.

The arrogance with which an entire art form, developed over the ages and representing the best of the human mind, as sophisticated as it is profound, is casually brushed off, is breathtaking, and can only be explained by the simple conclusion that a mind that is capable of such condescension must lack the musical faculty altogether. Meanwhile, it is very regrettable that this book is used as the starting point of teaching "new music" to uninitiated students. It contains much useful factual information about musical and sonic developments in the twentieth century, but it is put in a context which makes much of it quite meaningless. The quote is not an exception, a freakish blurb from a provincial country, but typical and representative of a way of thinking which only became acceptable in public space after the onset of modernism. Eventually it became the established way of thinking about new music in general and part of the curriculum of professional music education. So, before students have the chance to develop their own opinions on the basis of available musical facts, the context they are fed with is immediately wrong from the very start—how could they discover the reality of the musical tradition if musical facts are presented in a distorted way? De Leeuw's book, which absorbed the general international consensus within musical modernism, is comparable to the numerous writings of Boulez, Stockhausen, and others, and is symptomatic of a mindset which is determined to create a place for a new art form—but is unaware that in the process it is attacking a precious tradition because the new art form is placed at the wrong location. It is like demolishing a medieval cathedral in an old town center to make place for a glass-and-steel office block, instead of building this block (if it has to be built at all) in the outskirts where it would not destroy something of great value. And De Leeuw was not at all a fanatical, revolutionary character: he was a very serious, quiet man, with a beard and professorial glasses; a modest and mediocre sonic artist keeping his distance from the louder modernist discussions in the 1960s and enjoying the reputation of an intelligent and respectable teacher at the Amsterdam Conservatory. He did not represent a "fundamentalist" avant-garde position but instead a broad, institutionalized consensus in the new music establishment.

A tome of collected writings by Pierre Boulez, published in English under the misleadingly neutral title *Orientations* (Harvard University Press, 1986), is full of such serious misconceptions, adorned with quasi-scientific graphs and charts, and including a sneering chapter upon Beethoven as a symbol of the "outdated" European musical tradition. Like Iannis Xenakis in his "sonic" testament, *Formalized Music* (Pendragon Press, 1992), in which the author tries to translate musical and sonic phenomena into scientific terms, the reference to scientific methods—which, in the arts, seem to have been a fast-acting solvent of critical faculties—is supposed to give the impression that a "pure," "objective" grip upon "musical" materials is at hand. One would wish that the writings of Boulez and Xenakis had been exposed to the deconstructionist solvent of Derridian mirror games, in the way one combats one type of poison with another (Jacques Derrida: *Positions*, 1987; *Margins of Philosophy*, 1982). The lack of a sense of reality in a mental territory where only interpretation and projection reigns would have been an apt demonstration of the Derridian idea that there is no meaning, no reality, but only *texts* referring to other texts. Could it nonetheless be that Boulez's contributions as a sonic artist, a writer, a conductor, and a teacher have, somehow, exercized a positive influence upon cultural life? More probable is that they have done a lot of damage to both the reputation of the art of composing, of sonic art, and of conducting as well: the "new standards of clarity," which have been accepted by many other conductors in the wake of his performing activities, are more often than not applied to scores which ask for a much more subtle balancing and coloring. "Clarity" is not an objective quality which can be put into operation with any music. It is not surprising that the dryness of Boulez's work, and his performances of both music and sonic art earned him the nickname of *notre nouveau Saint-Saëns* in certain French circles.

One would think that the kind of writing that sees nothing unusual or negative in modernism has died out, but in the musical world there are still many people around who have not noticed any difference between music and sonic art, nor can they find anything negative in the drastic disruption which was modernism. It is a naive mindset which even can be found in specialized academe, as shown by the English musicologist Arnold Whittall, well known for his generous but often empty verbiage. His *Musical Composition in the Twentieth Century*, in an affected and roundabout prose, fully ignores the effects of modernist atonality, in spite of its introduction, which begins with a quote from the English composer Alexander Goehr, which could have given the author a clue or two:

> . . . a great deal of music written in the last seventy years or so [writing in the eighties, JB] cannot be regarded as a straightforward continuation of Classical and Romantic music, either in the way it is conceived or in the way it is meant to be listened to. Background-foreground perception [meant as references to other music or an established tradition, JB] is inapplicable here because, in reality, insufficient background is implied. Continuity is fragmented or constructed of events unrelated to each other, pitch succession too complex to be memorable, and constructional procedures too difficult to be perceived as aural logic. (Alexander Goehr, "Music as Communication," in *Finding the Key: Selected Writings of Alexander Goehr*, ed. D. Puffett, London 1998, p. 231, as quoted in: Arnold Whittall, *Musical Composition in the Twentieth Century*, Oxford University Press, New York, 1999.)

All this could be translated into: *A great deal of music written in the last seventy years or so is just very clumsy.* For the musical person, the quote is an apt description of sonic art, expressing Goehr's doubts about post-1945 "avant-gardism," to which he had an oblique relationship. In general he kept to the original ideas of modernism as formulated by Schönberg, first introducing them belatedly in traditionalist England, later on regretting it a bit and casting an envious eye upon people who were musically more gifted than he and upon past glories: "People like Brahms knew something which we have lost." This "something" was, of course, the understanding of the inner workings of musical energies within a tonal narrative and their expressive capacities. A rationalism, disconnected from this understanding, leads to a distortion of the art form and the projection upon music history of a materialist idea: the "line of progressiveness." A telling historicist example of where this kind of mentality can lead is Goehr's irritated advice to "grow up" to composition students who had the bad taste to show an occasional interest in composers like Schumann ("Schumannesque" being the most devastating critique Goehr held in reserve for composition students who had not fully understood Schönberg's notion of logic). Goehr also denied that there had been a suppression of contemporary tonal music by the modernist establishment, asserting that failed careers of postwar tonal composers were all due to individual circumstances and individual life stories, which is as much as saying that there is no forest but only very many separate, individual trees, or that there was no Second World War but very many separate, individual deeds of personal aggression.

Arnold Whittall, while writing up musical modernism, seems to have forgotten his earlier generalization about new music in the twentieth century:

> . . . the common conclusion is that the modern age, with its unprecedented social and national conflicts and its remarkable technological and intellectual advances, is simply not an age in which worthwhile art can be expected to flourish: it is too unstable, too diffused, and art reflects this without being able to transcend it—hence, in music, the emphasis on discord, fragmentation and sheer diversity of style. (*Music Since the First World War*, London, Dent, 1988, p. 1–2.)

One can only feel sorry for Bartok, Stravinsky, Prokofiev, Ravel, Szymanowski, Britten, and Shostakovich for not having lived up to Dr. Whittall's expectations. But one should not forget that academics who are more than willing to accept modernism on its own terms, searching for innocent material to subject to their prowess, often are not interested at all in the reality of the world. An apt demonstration of this mentality is Whittall's recent book: *Introduction to Serialism* (Cambridge, 2008), which can be considered a remarkable exercise in useless superfluity, with serialism being the most pointless, meaningless, amateuristic, destructive, and nonsensical endeavor the musical world has ever seen, an awareness that eventually even penetrated its most fiery advocates. (The activities of John Cage are here bypassed because they are not even endeavors.)

The idea that "modern music" was some kind of exploration of sound material by a professional community, like a well-organized scientific enterprise, led to the development of a jargon that gave the impression of sophisticated complexity. So, compositional processes were "elevated" to a quasi-analytical level where phenomena could be wrapped in a language which would suggest immense depth of meaning and objective intellectuality. A master in this genre was, of course, Pierre Boulez. In descriptions of contemporary structuralist problems, his labyrinthine prose reads like an attempt to disguise the blatantly obvious, in a quasi-complexity comparable with the products of medieval sophism. Here is a representative example where heterophony is described:

> There are two types of properties necessary for the formation of a heterophony: general properties which indicate the *placing,* and specific properties which result in the *production.* [. . .] Before entering into detail, heterophony must be precisely defined: it is a structural distribution of identical pitches, differentiated by divergent temporal co-ordinates, manifested by distinct intensities and timbres; as a result, the concept of heterophony will be extended from the monodic to the polyphonic level. (From: "Musical technique," in *Boulez on Music Today,* 1971, Faber & Faber; studies written in Darmstadt for Darmstadt, p. 121)

Translated, this merely says, "Notation is needed to read and to play the notes. Heterophony is combining structurally different layers of material with identical notes. In the result, monody becomes polyphony."

It is understandable that the opportunity of blowing up trivialities to quasi-scientific proportions attracts people who see in the creation of word mist an invitation to produce a theater of "profundity" with which to intimidate the group they envy and fear the most: that of professional musicians, who are practical people in the first place and otherwise too busy to theorize much in a purely rationalistic way about what they are doing, who have their talent and knowing intuition guiding them in the ambiguous territory of music. This does not mean that practical musicians are not intellectually gifted or interested. They merely know by experience the serious limitations of purely rational speculation in a field that is mainly determined by emotional, intuitive, and thus irrational forces. Musical talent is a product of the imagination, of the inner life, of what formerly was called "the soul"; a one-sided rationalistic approach is destructive in that field. Did Boulez never write something useful about music? No, he wrote perceptively about Berlioz, Wagner, Mahler, Debussy, and Stravinsky, but always from a structuralist point of view, which is alien to the artistic outlook of these composers. He treated his subject matter on a material level, mostly keeping the artistic/aesthetic context from which these composers created, at bay.

Recently, Boulez tried to soften his hard-edged image by drawing attention to his supposedly more humane intentions. According to an article in connection with an upcoming Boulezbian Weekend at the Southbank Centre in London, the former "musical terrorist" seemed to have had something of a conversion about musical ideals:

When I spoke to Boulez, during the rehearsals for the performances he will bring to London with the Ensemble Intercontemporain next week, he used words about his music you'd normally associate with composers of an earlier generation. He wanted "coherence"; he said his recent music was a kind of storytelling, and most surprisingly of all, he told me his music "expressed myself, simply that", including his emotional life and spirituality. (*The Guardian*, 22/9/2011)

What should we think of this when it is placed against the background of his sonic art? Either it was an attempt to also draw some *musical* audience to the festival apart from the small group of sonic art lovers, which must have been surprising considering what the audience was actually going to hear, or it was an embarrassing revelation of the state of Boulez's inner life. "Coherence" and "storytelling" has always been utterly and consistently absent in the listening experience of his work, and if it "expresses" himself—"simply" on top of that—and includes his "emotional life" and "spirituality," we can only feel sorry for the man on noticing the immense void thus exposed in his works.

We will discretely pass over the other "arch father" of musical modernism, Karlheinz Stockhausen, because in spite of his relative fame in the 1950s and 1960s, when he provided a wide range of sonic possibilities—even reaching into pop music spheres—interest in his work and writings dwindled during the last decades of the century when he withdrew into a megalomaniacal, new-agey fantasy world over which he tried to reign with total control. He found another way of disposing of past musical culture: he ignored it, which must not have been difficult, since his thinking had no cultural roots in it. Reading his many utterances about himself and his work, always from a structuralist point of view, one begins to understand why he hardly ever referred to music: he seems to never have noticed it.

An imitation of scientific and philosophical thinking can never replace musical activity, be it composing or performing. Who ever had the patience to sit through one of his very long "operas" that make up the cycle *Licht*, will find the longeurs of Wagner's *Ring* a welcome breeze of fresh air in comparison. It is the claim that this is supposed to be music, and operatic music on top of that, which turns it into an embarrassing demonstration of pretentious poverty. In spite of all the desperate attempts to make the so-called complexities (which turn out to be of the most naive sort) speak, the result is boredom and an offence to any cultured and intelligent person. Stockhausen's reaction to the 9/11 attack on New York was this: it was a "great work of art." This should not surprise us since it perfectly fitted his fantasy world, totally disconnected from reality and from morality.

Some musicologists, following the quasi-scientific recipe and getting wrapped up in their self-congratulatory prose, therefore fail to see the thing that is utterly obvious to anybody else; it shows how dangerous it is to enter a field in which one is not quite suited to maneuver given the nonconceptual nature of the art form. One needs a strongly developed musical intuition to be able to intellectually grasp what is really happening in this unstable and ambiguous territory, where maps have to be readjusted and corrected according to empirical evidence. Great mistakes of interpretation are therefore part and parcel of music theory, and so it comes as no surprise that important occurrences in music are often missed by theorists, like wandering tourists who don't notice the Grand Canyon because they have the wrong map, as the example of Arnold Whittall's writings shows. However, the support from academics for sonic art as a form of music has helped to open the gates to crowds of people who had nothing to seek in the field of musical composition, but who saw in sonic art an opportunity to play out the role of "composer," people who feverishly studied all the elements and materials of "avant-gardism," encouraged by the modernist academics, in the happy illusion that their activities were a kind of music. Using the historicist development model of progressiveness as presented by academia to secure their aesthetic position, they became eligible for the state subsidies which began to pour in, financial support intended to protect the avant-garde from the vagaries of a "conservative" music praxis and to help create the breeding ground for high art music in some unforeseeable future. The "expert" committees of subsidizing bodies, burdened with the responsibility of supporting new musical creation and helping great talents survive in a hostile world, more often than not consisted of people who would not hear more in classical music than a pet animal would—specialists who don't hear the music but only the sound it makes. And so the one incompetent dilettante kept the other upright, and most of the available money went to the fakes—as still quite a lot will go that direction.

One might ask oneself this: is it possible, is it conceivable, that so many seemingly intelligent, educated people spend their entire professional lives on a nonsensical subject—sound art *as music*—publishing books, essays, articles, and "composing" and performing things under the influence of a serious delusion, as if affected by a psychopathological condition, some sort of monstrous distortion of reality, and that all those products—being so-called "works of music" and writings about their philosophies and structuring—consecutively find their place in a cultural consensus, forming a subsidized musical establishment? Is this not stretching the contention too far to be credible? For the innocent reader who has no idea of the immense amount of nonsense that lies buried on the shelves, breaking under the weight of misdirected pretension, this may indeed seem a possibility. But history shows us, alas, that such collective mania are perfectly possible and sustainable over long periods. For instance, a short look into the political history of the last century should quench any such doubts.

As could be expected, many music critics played a dubious role in the creation of the *fata morgana* of modernism. In the 1950s and 1960s, the majority of music critics took a strong stand against modernism, but due to a lack of substantial arguments which could be used as a defense against the accusation of "conservatism," eventually many let themselves be persuaded, and, gradually, began to defend "musical progressiveness." The emerging *brave new world* advocated a mythical self-image of man as a strong, nonsentimental hero not hindered by sensitivity, subtlety, or civilized values like the "effeminate" susceptibility to beauty and emotional experience. Dissonant modernist "music," therefore, answered a need to appear tough, progressive, and strong, or, in short, heroic. It will be clear that this self-image stems from the same source as the "heroism" cultivated in fascism and communism: the logical and inevitable companion of barbarism—a boy scout machismo blown up to absurd proportions. For the community of music criticism, this image began to be attractive, with the consequence that "old-fashioned" music began to appear degenerate. A telling and embarrassing example can be found in a recent recollection of the English music critic Ivan Hewett, who had made a strong case for modernism in the last century:

> When I was just starting to explore classical music I naturally gave Chopin a try and had an instant aversion to him. Those melting runs and arabesques made me feel physically sick, and I instantly translated this "yuck" sensation into a moral judgment. Chopin just wasn't serious, certainly not compared to the tough modern music I favored. The music was too weirdly intense, but in a feeble way, as if it needed to lie down with a bottle of smelling salts. If pressed to say why I disliked it so much, I imagine I would have said it was too girlie. Music shouldn't be like that; it should have some backbone. (*Telegraph*, 29/4/10)

In this quote, after the typical arrogance of a certain type of professional music critics ("I gave Chopin a try"), we see how primitiveness in "music" was confused with "backbone," how ugliness and barbarism were understood as "strength," and how thoroughly *unmusical* such a stance was. Missing the profound strength and superb artistic qualities of Chopin's art (who wrote more than a couple of nocturnal arabesques) is a blunder of the first order. Sonic art could thus become the hobby horse of anybody who lacked musical understanding, and could give music critics the motivation to defend sonic artists, in whom they recognized some of their own mentality, in public space. We find the same images of modernist "heroism" in the debate in British contemporary architecture, where a strong and successfully emerging revival of classicism is criticized by the old modernist architectural community with arguments that seem to belong to the period of totalitarian regimes in Europe, which shows a comparable disdain for civilians, tradition, the past, and humanist values. As the English psychiatrist and cultural critic Theodore Dalrymple rightly noted in *Our Culture; What's Left of It* (2007): a rough culture produces rude people—the bad chases the good away if the good is not defended. And this is *not* a conservative, right-wing reactionary remark, but common sense, for anybody concerned about the survival of our civilization.

The art of serious composition requires a very rare musical talent, which in any period only a handful of people possess. More people active in writing serious music, but somewhat less gifted, come close to the level of these top artists, but their number is still quite low, certainly in comparison to talented painters. To be a *sonic* artist, however, *musical* talents are not required, and this explains the sheer number of "modern composers" and "composition students" everywhere in the Western world where sonic art has replaced the teaching of musical composition at conservatories and universities. The quasi-scientific outlook upon notions of "modern music" thus opened many doors to people who, in other periods, would never dream of a musical profession and would never be able to find credibility in the cultural field. In 1977, with the aim of mobilizing and channeling sonic interests, Pierre Boulez opened his "sonic science center" in Paris, in the cellar of the Centre Pompidou, thus creating a focus point as an alternative to the "decadent" central performance culture. In its early years, the *Institut de Recherche et Coordination Acoustique/ Musique* (IRCAM), together with its in-house Ensemble Intercontempo- rain—according to Alex Ross in his *The Rest is Noise*—consumed up to 70 percent of the French budget for contemporary music. Since then, this organization produced numerous "composers" who spread throughout the world, trying to carry out the great enterprise of the demolition of music as an art form. Like the inadequate neuroscientists who try to undo the notion of the human psyche as an old-fashioned romantic fairy tale, they attempt to have the idea of music replaced by sonicism, whereby quasi-scientific approaches take the place of musical considerations, thus getting rid of the "irrational forces" that have driven musical history for so long. Instead of presenting itself as a purely *sonic* research laboratory, IRCAM functions as an institution that tries to introduce sonic art as *music* into the cultural field instead of the purely scientific field, with the result that the musically challenged can cash the funds, which would be more effectively and justly spent on art music. IRCAM provides a platform for the musically untalented with musical pretentions, so it is no surprise that, in music life, the institute is sometimes referred to as the *Institute for the Retrograde Conservation of Abominable Musicians.*

The cult of sonic art has even spread—like a viral disease—to places which want to compete with the "latest" forms of modernity: Japan, South Korea, China, South America and soon, no doubt, in Kyrgyzstan, Sri Lanka, Dubai, and Gabon, as soon as the cultural exchange and funding programs are in place. The cause of this interest in Western musical modernism is, of course, the symbolism it carries of being "up-to-date" and "developed," of being part of the most progressive movements in the world, and, ironically, this makes modernist music part of the same superficial and global media culture, with its TV shows, cell phones, hairdos and pop Americana, against which modernism initially was a strong reaction. It has all greatly contributed to the consensus, in the central performing culture where still high standards of artistic creation are more or less in place, that *any* new music must be bad, ugly, and incompetent, and, for that reason, superfluous.

Next to sonic art and the American reaction to it: process music, a third type of "new music," can be heard here and there, a productive activity with roots in the 1960s, which also has its claims upon "music" but which hovers between vague reminiscences of European art music, pop music, and references to music of non-European cultures which go under the heading of "world music." It is a mix, like a soup of leftovers, of different ingredients from different sources but without the craft of the original sources and without context of a tradition—and thus, without much identity or character of its own. Often it is very primitive, and sometimes—if a bit more sophisticated—the sound world of Hollywood film music is not very far off. And because it is much less offensive to the ear than modernism, it is sometimes welcomed in concert life as a happy alternative, where it is preferred as harmless insignificance to the invasive disruption of modernism. Because the different stylistic fields from which this is eclectically chosen tend to neutralize each other, the results are mostly mediocre and nicely insignificant at best, and primitive and inane at worst. Because its "composers" often find the central performance culture firmly closed to them, they set up their own little ensemble, mostly with an incongruous combination of instruments, and try to find inconspicuous and "unconventional" venues to confront something of an audience with their homework. With all due respect, it is quite surprising that so many young people who have grown up with pop music somehow feel the stirrings of more serious musical creativity and decide for a career as a composer, while ignoring the presence of such a rich musical tradition at their doorstep. They prefer the desert of primitivism to the sumptuous garden of creativity, sophistication, meaning, depth, and beauty to which the gates stand wide open. However, the myth of modernity with imagined closed doors prevents them from entering this territory, like the peasant who does not dare to enter the public library: "it is not for me." Instead of working at real craftsmanship, they prefer the easy-going, immediate, and superficial. Under the delusion that the help of electronic equipment will open the doors of musical invention, they cannot produce more than—at best—insignificant decoration without artistry and without interest. If musical composition were that easy, everybody would be doing it, and indeed the breed is popping up everywhere. Is this a problem? As long as it is considered a harmless hobby, there would be nothing against it; but unfortunately these activities are increasingly seen as something artistically professional. The danger is that well-meaning, innocent listeners will become misinformed about the art form and might find it more difficult to acquire *musical* understanding, which is conditional for a living musical culture. As a reflection of the spirit of a consumerist society, which has lost its understanding of its own high culture, this phenomenon is instructive, especially when it is mixed with pubescent "protests" against the wrongs in this world, like the works of Louis Andriessen that are—unsurprisingly—much appreciated by audiences who find listening to art music as difficult and challenging as children being forced to read Proust. (Andriessen, incidentally, is a typical example of the ideal official, state-supported antibourgeois revolutionary: cushioned with generous subsidies, which are paid for by the same "bourgeois society" that Andriessen attacks in his works with gruesome themes, he is given to regularly fulminate against the central performance culture, with its "bourgeois dead composers" and "dead values," cultivating a utopian dreamland where a teenage anger combines the spirit of totalitarianism, Calvinism, and destructiveness in a "music" in which hard, machine-like inevitability celebrates the emptiness of immaturity. Its fake "revolutionary spirit" is bourgeois through-and-through, like the vandalism of the spoiled children of 1968 which was possible because of the financial support of their hardworking parents.) But the products of this trend, representing neither music nor sound art, are a perfect example of what happens if a mind wants to be free and individual *before* having acquired the means of discrimination, craftsmanship, and artistic development. As we will see in chapters 5, 6, and 7, individual freedom and artistic expression is only possible against the background of a developed artistic tradition.

However, non-Western musical traditions can offer fertile ground for development, if handled by composers with real musical talent, who understand both the craftsmanship needed for the task and the underlying values of these traditions. In terms of tonality, rhetoric narrative, range of expression, and notational expertise, Western/European classical music (i.e., the classical tradition) is obviously superior to any non-Western musical tradition. But in restricted areas like rhythm, sound color, atmosphere, and spirituality, non-Western music may—in specific cases—be superior to Western music. To state that the Western classical tradition is superior to other traditions is not necessarily cultural imperialism, but can be a statement of fact, for which Westerners should not be ashamed of if supported by evidence. Navigating in this territory where the different frameworks of value and meaning of East and West overlap or clash can have negative consequences, as many of the late works by Messiaen show—works which try to combine Eastern and Western elements, lacking both the Eastern subtleties and the expressive and narrative range of Western traditions. An interesting example of East/West combinations that turns out well is the music of the Iranian/American composer Reza Vali, who uses tonal material and structures of his culture of origin but transforms them into an expressive language, rooted in Western narrative rhetoric and tonal argument. In contrast to the works by Messiaen, as mentioned, the result combines the best of two worlds (see chapter 9: "Some Composers," for more information about Vali).

Modernism made quite a cult of the notion of originality. By creating outrageously dissonant and chaotic sound art, originality standards of the new art form were supposed to be firmly established, since, in the beginning, nothing sounded like it. Of course originality has nothing to do with artistic quality. "Originality" is, in fact, not an aesthetic or artistic category but a psychological one. A work of art will automatically receive the personal fingerprints of the maker, if he or she has any personality. However, the longing to do or to say something that has never before been said is as old as civilization: in about 2000 B.C., the Egyptian scribe Khakheperresenb was already voicing what could be called the eternal complaint of individuality: "Would I had phrases that are not known," the scribe laments, "in new language that has not been used, with not an utterance which has grown stale, which men of old have spoken." There is always a tension between common practice and the urge of the individual to express himself in a personal way. If he creates his own totally self-referential language, nobody will understand him; if he repeats exactly what other people have said, his utterance is pointless. But in the margin between a common vocabulary and the individual point of view, real originality can be found, which expresses itself not in the vocabulary itself but in the way it is used: there is the distinction between the level of the material and the level of meaning and expression. The notion of originality as cultivated by modernism was primitive because, following a recipe of sufficient doses of structuralism, complexity, and dissonance, did not create originality, but an easy conformism: do the original thing that everybody else is doing. The personal imprint upon the material is a much more subtle and sophisticated phenomenon and is only discernible after understanding in which direction it can be found. One thinks of the early critique that Bernard Shaw leveled against Brahms: he heard merely bits of Beethoven, Schubert, and Schumann in passing, and only later in life did he understand the strongly personal treatment of this utterly original and nonconformist composer — nonconformist because neither did he follow the fashionable trend of romanticist cultivation of impulsive expression, pumped up chromaticism, and striking instrumental colorings, nor the fixed formulae of classicist theorists. The misunderstandings around "originality" and "personality" have not only blinded the advocates of modernism toward new classical music ("it is only an imitative repetition of what has already been said") but also toward the products of modernism itself: in that territory, dogmatic conformism, and bland conventionality finds their culminating apotheosis.

An interesting side effect of the urge to be "modern" or "of this time" is the immature wish that the world is "mine"; like a spoiled child who wants the environment adapted to its immediate and unconsidered needs. Recently a "modern composer" said in a TV interview that he wholeheartedly disliked old things—antiques, old buildings, or an old church for instance: "That is not my world, these things are hostile toward me, they say to me that I do not belong to them. I am of my own world, the world of now, and that is what I want to express." The music heard afterward fully confirmed what this world had to say, which amounted to next to nothing. The poor man did not say that he was *intimidated*, which would indicate an awareness of quality, but that he experienced *hostility*, which can only be explained as a projection of his own hostility toward a world that could, in all artistic respects, be superior: to allow this awareness to sink in would not stimulate development and learning, but would destroy a vulnerable ego that wanted to protect itself against challenges too great to cope with. Such a man should never become an artist.

The achievements of the past are a structural part of our world, and are there to be understood, to be learned from; and learning requires a certain modesty and awareness of the intentions of our forbearers whose presence in their works should support us, not threaten us. Cutting off the spiritual bridge to the generations that came before us robs us of learning trajectories, which is disastrous in the field of serious art. This is the way in which modernist ideologies of progressiveness cultivated immaturity, laziness, and incompetence and became an instrument of protection of the talentless against being measured up to real artistic achievements. No wonder new music is in deep trouble; it has lost its anchors and has now been adrift for half a century.

The problems of contemporary music cannot be solved within the "modern circuit" of specialized concerts and festivals, but have to be addressed in the context of the central performance culture and in relation to its fundamental principles of musicality and all they imply. The first stage of a solution should be a clear understanding of the meaning of musical modernism, which cannot be obtained from within the circles of new music where sonic art is accepted as normal: a philosophical position outside that box is a prerequisite for seeing the nature of the problem. To many people, the repertoire of the central performance culture seems, because of the claims of sonic art, to be without any real successor in the present. If sonic art had its rightful place as an *alternative* art form, next to music—like photography and conceptualism next to painting—the cultural field might be extended by such varied offers of contrasting experience. But the claims of modernist ideologies, which are still implied by many established institutions for "new music," undermine any credibility it otherwise might have had, however small, and turn sonic art into a tragic farce.

FOUR
Temples of Delight: How Not to Build a Concert Hall

Sonic art is best enjoyed in the context of sonic concerts by specialist ensembles and soloists—if possible in a hall where all references to a *musical* culture are absent so that sonic art can be enjoyed without the painful recollections of music and all the symbolism they may carry. Only in an environment where all spaces and materials are in harmony with the *brave new world* which sonic art represents can its works come fully into their own. This has been accomplished wonderfully in Amsterdam, where the most important hall for the central performance culture is the well-known traditional *Concertgebouw* ("Concert Building"), and where most sonic art finds an appropriate home in the new *Muziekgebouw* ("Music Building")—named as a "twin" of the Concertgebouw, still under the impression that sonic art was a form of music. For our subject, it is interesting to look into the history of the Muziekgebouw because it is one of the most recently built, large-scale concert halls in Europe specially destined for new music, characterizing the place of sonic art within the broader context of modernity and its relation to the past. In this sense it is comparable with the Parisian "Cité de la Musique" and other halls specially built for "new music."

When it was felt, in the 1960s and 1970s, that sonic art—because of its unpopularity in concert life—needed a permanent performance venue of its own in Amsterdam, a tiny concert space was opened behind a café at the quay of the river Amstel in 1979. This was a historic nineteenth-century structure and ironically, it was built in a vaguely classical style by the architect of the famous Concertgebouw, Adolf Leonard van Gendt. The complex of café and concert hall was called "De IJsbreker" (The Icebreaker), after the original purpose of the location, which housed the equipment for breaking the ice on the Amstel from the seventeenth century onward, the river being an important transport route for the city's *raison d'être*: trading and business.

After decennia of intense campaigning, the director of the IJsbreker, Jan Wolff, saw his (and modernist advocates') burning wish for a concert hall for new music fulfilled in 2005, when a purpose-built complex was opened right at the IJ (pronounced: "eye"), the broad river and harbor of Amsterdam. As we know, modernist architects are brilliant in designing precisely the right spaces which the purpose of the building deserves (as long as it fits within the context of the *Brave New World*) and especially in buildings destined for contemporary art can they invest all their invention to find the best suited symbolism for the performances (if the purpose is music) or collections (in case of museums); we have only to think of the Parisian *Centre Pompidou* or the *Museum für Moderne Kunst* in Frankfurt to know beyond doubt that modernism, as a mentality, forms an aesthetic and philosophical unity beyond the boundaries of genre. (Recently, the director of London's Tate Modern museum offended the intelligence of future visitors of the *Centre Pompidou* in a TV documentary by paternalistically stating that this museum was a "truly democratic" building because you could enter the exhibition spaces via escalators—how wonderful!)

The Amsterdam *Muziekgebouw*, built by the Danish architects Nielsen, Nielsen, & Nielsen (for triple assurance concerning unity of design?) is not an exception to the modernist aesthetic. Every aspect of this building, from its location to its structure and style, is perfectly conceived for the enjoyment of sonic art—apart from the financial disappointment that occurred when the city paid for the building but then refused to provide funds for the programming, with the result that only subsidized performance bodies could present themselves there: they have to hire the hall. The running of a big building for sonic art without a budget for programming forced the board to also accept *musical* performances, so an occasional baroque consort or classical chamber orchestra, next to world music and jazz performances, diluted the original purpose, but that is considered a minor setback. The building itself, located at one of the most inhospitable and inaccessible spots in the city, squeezed between the water of the IJ on one side and train rails and a busy motorway on the other, combines the grave minimalism of a crematorium with the industrial grand gestures of an airport hangar. The main entrance on the ground floor can only be reached via a long detour, but a big footbridge brings the courageous sonic listener from the tram stop at the motorway over a deep abyss to a revolving door on the first floor, opening to a big, unprocessed and plain cement wall. It is obvious that the visitor is to leave all stimulation of the senses behind. But that is not all: the big hall, containing 750 seats, has no interior design at all but is a cubical space confined by fence-like walls imitating the inside of a poultry house, with strips alternating with openings which can be illuminated in different bright

colors, as to create an appropriate atmosphere for the production presented. The acoustics can be changed by a movable ceiling, as can the size of
the podium. Seating area and podium can be put in different sizes, locations, and combinations. So, no parameter of the hall is stable (as comparable to sonic art), and no object has any character, like the surfaces which
consist mainly of glass, concrete, steel and—by way of exception—a
wooden floor in the most neutral grey-brown color. The building is completely void of any sign remotely reminiscent of artistic activity. Even the
tables and chairs in the café space show minimalistic form: the place is a
riot of monotonous and colorless functionalism. In the foyer, the enormous glass walls open up to the vistas of the IJ and a windy, unadorned
terrace. This view is the only one worth giving some visual attention and
thus typically represents something *outside* the complex. The absence of
any plant, however tiny, inside and outside the building, adds to the
impression of almost absolute artificiality. It must be granted that the
acoustics are good; yet, the entire complex and location breathe one single thing: *abstraction*. It is a thoroughly bare place, denying the entire
dimension of the inner life fed by the senses.

Did all the participants in the planning process suffer from cerebral
death while contemplating the ambitious possibilities of "creating the
ultimate concert hall of the twenty-first century," as the initiative was
called? No—instinctively they were drawn, at each step of the planning
trajectory, toward the solution which would create the best possible environment for sonic art, which means avoiding precisely the things that are
most loathed in the sonic art universe: the "naive taste" of the bourgeoisie; the kitsch of "classical glamor," both in architectural representation
and celebration of "stardom"; any reference to the past; and all the trap-
pings of Adorno's famous concept of "false consciousness," which leads
the listener away from the truth of art. What is it then, this truth? The
message of the building seems to be that the listener is given the promise
to fly loose from the banal world where the decadent past still has a
stronghold, to enter the sphere of pure sound where he or she will enjoy,
through the pinnacles of sonic art, an acoustical dream of purity, where
he or she will no longer be hindered by the painful burden of the emotional dimensions of human life. It will be clear that this message is fully
in tune with the dehumanizing tendencies of the last century. In fact the
building expresses a thoroughly conventional and conservative modernism, an attempt to break as completely as possible with the premodernist
past, avoiding any possible reference to art, to music, to the senses, to
nature, concentrating on "pure functionality," but thereby cocooning itself into a time capsule of modernist 1960s idealism. It could not be a
better place for established, subsidized sonic art and, in fact, as such it is a
museum. The irony is, of course, that in this kind of place the art for
which the hall has been built represents as much a *museum culture* as the
central performance culture, with the difference that the latter offers

much more artistic substance and cultural significance, plus a far greater potential for development, than the temples of sonic art.

Fortunately, nowadays experts can devise the best possible acoustics, where the main function of the building is to create the best possible space for orchestral and chamber music performances. But the acoustical aspect and the practicality of performing/seating spaces are not the only functions of a concert hall. The character of the building is important, too, because it has to create an atmosphere removed from ordinary daily life, preparing the visitor for the experience of interiority which awaits him or her. The elaborate decorations that we find in the famous classical concert halls, like the Viennese Musikverein and the Amsterdam Concertgebouw, serve two functions: first, by dispersing and harmonizing the sound like a large musical instrument, and second, in creating the right emotional and psychological atmosphere for the audience. The many ornaments perfectly fulfill these two requirements—in a time when acoustical science was still quite undeveloped. Modern concert halls, although they may achieve success as to the acoustical requirement, in their aesthetic realization there is very often much to be wished for, because as the average modern aesthetic is perfect for *sonic* art, it is very poorly suited to a space destined for *musical* performances. Even where a certain minimal dignity is achieved, as in the recent Bridgewater Hall in Manchester, an innocent visitor entering the building would not be sure whether it were city council premises, a banking office, a hospital, a hotel, or a conference center. The Royal Festival Hall in London could, together with the Barbican Hall with its labyrinthine entrance trajectories, be considered further informative examples of the failure of modernist architects to invent spaces for classical music, which results from the mental world that modernism inhabits: as soon as the purpose of the building is something related to interiority or spirituality, like a concert hall or a church, most modernist architects' brains seem to fall apart.

In the last century, the notion of functionality has been mainly understood as material, practical functionality. Architectural histories from the 1950s and 1960s, for example, often express a morally driven disapproval of the elaborate ornamentation of Roman, late Gothic, or Baroque architecture, condemning such efforts as a waste of material and energies with the definitive denunciation of being "nonfunctional." But of every building in which humans dwell, be it the home, the workplace, or places for religious services or cultural activities, the most important function is to create the right—i.e., the psychologically and aesthetically best possible— atmosphere and character. A building always *says* something, independent of whether its designer has intended it or not. It gives character to a place, a location, a spatial area. And this character influences the people dwelling in it. The grandeur and poetry of the central Parisian cityscape, the ruined pomposity of Rome, the floating dreams of Venice, and the picturesque and humane center of Amsterdam offer visual stimuli inviting identification, and in this way transfer something of their "message" to the viewer. It seems therefore natural that typical modernist quarters in big cities have a high crime rate, for the "message" of their buildings often refers to meaninglessness, emptiness, alienation, isolation, boredom, infinite sadness, and hopelessness. There are not many things as demoralizing as the sight of a concrete wall in the rain. Also the spectacular modernist public projects, intended to express local "progressive modernity" by whatever means, cannot help but alienate the civilians who still maintain a residue of civilized values, while tickling the exhibitionist lust of bureaucrats to leave an imprint of their utopian ambitions on the earth's surface. A telling practitioner of these neomodernist excesses is, no doubt, Anglo-Iranian architect Zaha Hadid, who, with her impractical and mostly aborted plans, which tellingly can only exist in virtual computer space unhindered by reality, regularly explodes her building budgets with personal fees in the millions, thereby showing that selling wet dreams to culturally handicapped civil servants is really good business.

In contemporary architecture, over the last decennia, a slow but steady revival of classicism has emerged, comparable to the revival of figurative painting. Its early pioneers have been the Luxembourger Leon Krier and the Englishman Quinlan Terry (both sporting a track record of defamation, ridicule, and accusations of "kitsch" and "pastiche" from modernist colleagues), and the other "extremists" Greek/English Demetri Poryphorios and the American Allan Greenberg. Prince Charles has made a strong case with his critique upon modernist architecture. The negative reactions he encountered from the architectural establishment—where modernism and postmodernism have become the conformist bottom line—are yet another proof of the historicist thinking of modernism in all its forms. Ironically, new classical buildings look "historic" but are in fact ahistorical, because they are based upon timeless and universal aesthetic principles (which is something different from definitions of style). Modernist buildings are historic through and through, as they want to consciously express "modern times."

All arts, including architecture for the public space, make use of design and style, and (as we have seen) thus use instruments of expression, intentionally or unintentionally. It is interesting to visualize comparable solutions when one looks into the stylistic problems encountered by contemporary classicist architects because they are quite similar to those of contemporary classicist composers. Is using a style from the past necessarily pastiche or kitsch? Will building in a classical style necessarily result in some kind of replica? How can examples be further developed without distorting the basic principles of style and aesthetics? How are inner inconsistencies treated? What is the relationship between structure and expression?

It is clear that the type of explorative questions within new classicism, in whatever art form, are fundamentally different from those within modernism. Ironically, modernist critique upon new-classical architecture operates from an entirely inadequate point of view because the fundamental considerations on which classicism is based are not understood. The critique falls into two categories: first, classicism has no connection to the modern world and is thus not viable; second, its products have no originality but are lame copies of examples from the eighteenth century or earlier. Of course, it is possible to badly build in one style or another, but the margin of freedom offered by the classical repertoire is considerable, as is the variety of application for any conceivable purpose. The second objection is invalid since the idea that classicism as such can only "repeat" designs ignores the obvious fact that the quality of any design is dependent upon the talent and imagination of the architect in question; it says nothing about the style as such. The first objection is more serious, and it shows the modernist bias that art and architecture should be the expression of the modern world, which is the common historicist notion of projecting a "line of development" from the past into the future. We have seen in chapters 2 and 3 that this kind of thinking has no foundation in artistic practice and can be compared with utopian ideologies like communism and fascism, with their totalitarian prescriptions and rewriting of history.

When we look at the designs of the mentioned architects, we are at first struck by the sheer beauty and harmony of the designs and the perfection of craftsmanship. Indeed the link with the timeless beauty of the past is obvious. The accusation of "repetition" has no ground, since within a classicist tradition, development rests upon imitation and the small personal deviations from custom: artistic and aesthetic quality is something different from originality. The buildings of Michelangelo are not admired for their originality but for their artistic quality, which is a different category. Where his personal quirks were imitated, as in later mannerist architecture by, for example, Giorgio Vasari, artistic quality was not the immediate inevitable result. And in the Baroque period we find examples of originality which are less than satisfactory, in spite of the utterly personal design (Palazzo Carignano and the Basilica of Superga in Turin, the interior of Dresden's Frauenkirche). The accusation of "repetition" also shows ignorance of architectural history, where well-tried examples fostered an immense range of varied progeny; the extreme fear of imitation which runs through all art of the last century is neurotic and has nothing to do with a normal development of a cultural tradition.

But one would indeed wish that Terry, Poryphorios, and Greenberg would show a bit more personal freedom in their designs, as we find with sixteenth- and seventeenth-century architecture. Their work seems to be focusing upon purety rather than personal expression, and this is understandable for architecture that is indeed a rebirth of a lost practice. Also the first buildings of Italian renaissance architecture show the same kind of search for harmony and purity, in an effort to recapture the balanced, inner qualities of the achievements of Antiquity. Renaissance architects like Alberti and Brunelleschi were not just trying to pick up the "grammar" of an old style, but wanted above all to recapture the *spirit* of classicism: its balance, its subtle relationships between design and mass, the way spaces were distributed, and the effect of harmonious grandeur. A realization, different from the Romans, and thus deviating from the models, was often the result of practical circumstances. For instance, the requirements of building a Christian church were very different from those of a Roman bath or temple; thus the aesthetics of Antiquity had to be translated into a new context, had to be made contemporary, not intentionally (to be "modern"), but simply because the practical requirements were different. The results could thus not be the same as the Roman buildings. In the same way, classical architecture for the twenty-first century will have, even in its attempts to closely follow historical examples, different results, as can be seen in the "Palladian" office building at London's Tottenham Court Road (numbers 264–267), created by Quinlan and Francis Terry. One could even think of a classically styled mosque to express a Europeanized Islam, which would give off a powerful message to Muslim immigrants: your religion is welcome in the West, but should be adapted.

Meanwhile, new classicism in contemporary architecture, which has up until now mostly found realizations in the Anglo-Saxon world, is nothing less than a miracle. The amazing fact that such a complex and sophisticated aesthetic can indeed be recaptured nowadays, in a time when this is—among professionals—a grave taboo, shows that a tradition is not a museum object but a wavelength of creative fantasy, which can be reached through study and loving dedication. New classical architecture, with its associations with humanism, democracy, the human scale, beauty, and its numerous ties with a glorious architectural past, expresses the essence of European civilization and the richness of its creativity reaching back to its early beginnings by the brilliant Greeks. Nothing seems more viable as an expression of the present time than a return to aesthetic values which have served our culture so well and so long in the past, and it goes without saying that new classical music forms a natural part of this urge to find expressive and aesthetic value capable of defining and expressing European cultural identity and the European creative spirit.

From all this, it is not difficult to conclude that architecture for new concert halls *for music* should refrain from modernism, learn from history, and follow the examples of the classical buildings which have proven to be so successful not only in terms of acoustics, but also in terms of their visual character. As far as style is concerned, classicist designs seem best suited for music performances, being very flexible and combining the impression of worldly loftiness with human scale and proportion. The message of a classicist design would be that the tradition which has given European civilization its most characteristic longterm flavor, from old-Greek times onward, would be taken up again and revived; it would reinforce a positive sense of cultural identity and continuity. For musical concert halls, a classicist building would be best, as the modernist variety would do sonic concerts the best service. It goes without saying that designing a new, classicist concert hall would challenge the architect's faculties of invention, especially in relation to ornamentation—but given the riches of historical examples, there is enough to explore, to reinterpret, to develop variations for contemporary purposes in the same spirit as the composers of new classical music explore their examples and find new forms for them.

FIVE

The Enduring Presence of the Past

If we put the last century's notions of "old" and "new" in a broader historic perspective, it becomes clear how short-sighted these notions were and how wrong it was to give them an aura of absoluteness, since these notions are, by their very nature, relative and flexible, and dependent upon context. When the painter, architect, and theorist Giorgio Vasari wrote his *Lives of the Great Artists* (1568), a collection of biographies of Italian artists, he related the developments of recent and contemporary art to comparable developments in antiquity that he considered reborn in the present. The rediscovery of the culture of antiquity as a source of inspiration and as a standard of quality was felt, in Renaissance times, as something new and dynamic. The influence of the culture of antiquity can be traced back to the twelfth century, when conditions favored a more refined and sophisticated civilization. This was not the first wave of Renaissance thinking, for Charlemagne had already stimulated interest in antiquity in the early ninth century, in a spirit of constructive reform, after the worst of the barbarism of the seventh and eighth centuries had subsided. Later on, in the medieval world, Italy's culture was dominated by northern and eastern influences, and for many people at that time, "modern" meant the latest developments of medieval culture imported from the prosperous north, especially Flanders. The concept of a "modernity," based upon ideas from ages ago, was still controversial, but for the intelligentsia the works of poetry, science, and the visual arts of the Greco-Roman world were all superior to anything produced by contemporary culture. The presence of Roman monuments, mostly ruined, reminded the Italians of a glorious past and inspired them to dream of a possibly comparable future.

The Renaissance interest in antiquity as a civilizing influence is something fundamentally different from modern thinking. In the twentieth century, progress was understood as a confident leap into the future: a projected utopia, only made possible by a drastic break with the past. The Past stood for Reaction, and the Future for Progress. By comparison, the ideas of the artists of the Italian Renaissance give us an opposite picture. Although the relatively immediate past—the Middle Ages (also known as the Dark Ages)—was felt to have been stagnant, the future held the possibility of recreating a distant past from a mythological era, which had already profoundly influenced European intelligentsia. This potential recreation was considered something much better than the art of the Dark Ages, when the arts and crafts of Antiquity had eroded and their secrets had been lost.

Assuming that Vasari's view of the developments he describes reflected a broader consensus among the intellectual and artistic elite of his time, it is clear that the driving force behind the changes in the arts and architecture from the beginning of the Renaissance onward was due to an urge to do things *better* than before, not to be more *advanced* in the sense of being "more modern" and *for that reason* "better." Vasari clearly sees "early" artists like Cimabue, Giotto, and Simone Martini as still rather awkward, trying their best, and achieving the best that was possible in their time, but beginning an upward line through Lorenzo Ghiberti, Filippo Brunelleschi, and Sandro Botticelli to the "perfection" of his own time with brilliant people like Michelangelo, Tiziano, and Raphaello. So, in Renaissance times, being modern was the result of being better, while in the twentieth century, being better was the result of being modern. It may be clear that the latter idea is nonsensical because it rests upon an assumed historical position, while in the Renaissance "being better" was achieved through artistic quality, an attitude that was not incompatible with "looking back," if in earlier times, sources of inspiration and great examples could be found. An expression like Arthur Rimbaud's "Il faut être absolument moderne" would be unthinkable in the sixteenth century, because it expresses a historicist intention *prior* to the creation of the work of art.

Was the Italian and, in general, the European Renaissance a reactionary and backward-looking, and thus a conservative period, with all the associations of dullness and conventionality? As we know, the opposite is true: this incredibly rich period meant the flowering of a spirit of invention and aesthetic sensibility. This lasted until the nineteenth century, when this broad wave of inspiration-by-antiquity found a premature death through its codification in academic institutions, in a society that was changing fast in the industrial revolution, and in the development of the bourgeoisie as the main territory of cultural action. The rebellion against a petrified academic culture was the cradle of modernism: the creative forces of life had left the territory of "official culture," which had suffocated innovation, and moved toward the margins of society, where neglected artists struggled to find new and freer ways of expression. The idea of "modern art," reflecting contemporary life instead of idealized subjects, was born from dissatisfaction with a tradition that was codified, frozen in prescriptions of outward appearances of style and form, and thus had become superficial and untrue.

Thus, in the nineteenth century, the urge of leaving conventional ideas about art behind got the label "modern." Since that trend eventually ended up in the dead-end street of establishment modernism, the word "modern" no longer fits this urge, which, incidentally, also lies behind the motivation of new classical composers: what they felt was "conventional" was called "modern" in the past century. A good example which shows that being "modern" in the period before modernism did not involve the need to destroy the fundamentals of the art form is the work of Debussy, who created an oeuvre which was shockingly untraditional in its own time, therefore very controversial. Debussy is often described as one of the "forefathers" of modernism, who (together with Schönberg) destroyed the orthodoxies of tradition and created a new and free musical paradigm. Boulez especially tried to show that some of the roots of his own sonic art were to be found in Debussy's explorations, but Debussy never destroyed the inner workings of tonality and the underlying dynamics of tradition, with their varied ways of achieving expression. In *The Cambridge Companion to Debussy* (Cambridge University Press, 2003), Boyd Pommeroy writes:

> In keeping with the progressive spirit of the new century, Debussy succeeded in forging elements from the tonal practice of his predecessors into something radically new. At the same time, his tonal language, even at its least orthodox, never loses sight of the traditional principles that ultimately give it meaning. In Debussy's music, tonal and formal processes continue to interrelate in ways not so fundamentally different from the tonal masterpieces of the preceding two centuries. To the extent that so vital an engagement with the tonal tradition went hand in hand with the creation of such strange and wonderful new sound-worlds, whose vivid modernity remains undimmed at the turn of another century, his achievement was perhaps unique (p. 177–78).

Because Debussy never destroyed the fundamentals of music, his work proved immensely influential for composers who were looking for new paths to explore but wanted to avoid the deadlock of atonalism. As in the work of Stravinsky, it is the superb *tonal* sense that makes the expressive power of this music possible; it is no coincidence that the later works of Stravinsky, when he was influenced by the modernist trends of the 1950s, are considerably less interesting. Like the great artists of the Italian Renaissance, Debussy was inspired by a dream of another world. But in his case, it was not the stimulating nostalgia for Antiquity, which for him stood for academic and "thus" dusty art forms; he detested everything "classical," in music, painting, and architecture. Nonetheless, his artistic temperament was classical through and through: perfectly balanced proportions, moderation in terms of expression, precise and concise craftsmanship, aristocratic style, and avoidance of everything cheap and vulgar. And, like the Renaissance artists who did not approach the art of Antiquity academically, he never undermined the mimetic basis of the art form. Contrary to that, he enriched it immensely and showed that freedom from classical forms could still preserve their spirit, as is eloquently shown in pieces like *Hommage à Rameau, Mouvement*, the symphonic *La Mer*, and, of course, the three late *Sonates*. In various articles and interviews, Debussy often mentioned the necessity of returning to the finesse and clarity of the French Baroque, which, for the French, is their *Grand Siècle* of classicism. Looking backward can easily go together with highly original creation because the process of interpretation operates on another level than the used style or materials; a really creative talent finds ways of combining elements from these two different levels in ever changing syntheses. One could raise this question: if this is so, could the musical modernism from the 1950s and 1960s then not serve as material for contemporary interpretation? Could the work of Boulez and Stockhausen not fulfill the same role as antiquity did for the Italian Renaissance artists? As we have seen, atonal music is not music but sonic art. And indeed, there are young contemporary sound artists who, within the field of sonic art, focus upon that period. They call their work "new complexity." The irony is that last century's modernism cannot turn into a thing of the past without losing its identity, because it wanted so desperately to embody the future. Like the glass and steel cubes of modernist buildings, it cannot afford to become old, to become the past, because that is totally undermining its *raison d'être*. When the future becomes the past, the one cancels out the other and the result is emptiness. New complexity is an excellent example of contemporary conservatism, since that is the only element that is left: the conservation of an idea.

The same landscape may reveal very different aspects, depending upon the position from which it is perceived. Also, the past can take on different meanings, changing with the perspective we choose. Marguerite Yourcenar, author of the celebrated historical novel *Memoirs of Hadrian*, was well aware of the ambiguities of historical perception. She commented in a late interview:

> If we look at history closely and attentively, leaving behind the academic and ideological clichés of our time, we conclude that every period, every milieu, had its own way of interpreting life. Although the human emotions are always more or less the same, made up of a certain restricted number of basic elements, they are open to thousands of variations, thousands of possibilities like the immensity of musical expression can be related back to the seven notes of the scale. You see these possibilities not only taking shape from century to century, but from year to year. After all, we don't think the same as in 1950 any

longer. It is fascinating to find at a precise date in the past, the way in which problems have presented themselves, our problems, or problems parallel to ours. In this way, history is a school of liberation. It liberates us from a number of our prejudices and teaches us to see our own problems and our own routines in a different perspective. . . . The past does not offer us an escape route, but a series of junctions, of different exits along the same way. If it may look as a form of escapism, it is an escape in the form of a leap of faith. Let me explain: the study of texts from antiquity has been such a stimulating leap of faith for Renaissance man, saturated as he was with medieval scholastic thought. The study of the Middle Ages was—up to a certain point—an inspiring "escape" for the romantic generation, bringing it back to the sources of popular poetry, to the original, European phenomenon, after the clarity, but also dryness, of the 18th century. (Patrick de Rosbo, *Entretiens radiophoniques avec Marguerite Yourcenar*, Mercure de France, 1972, p. 43–45; see further readings)

In periods of change, a civilization needs to draw on experience, as embodied in its cultural and intellectual inheritance, to be able to distinguish between irrelevant surface phenomena and meaningful developments. Engagement with the riches of a culture is not a formula but a learning trajectory of achievements of the human mind which may teach us what is right, what is good, what is meaningful and why, and in which context. It is a learning process which develops our capacity to make value judgments, without which no meaning can be found. Achievements from past periods have to be preserved, kept alive in their function of intellectual and cultural resources, so that they can be used and learned from when facing the challenges of the present. If the past is well understood, it will throw a light upon the world in which we live, a world that has long roots in the accumulated life experiences of numerous generations. The survival of this experience makes renewal possible, which is the "injection" of life into inherited forms and concepts. Creative innovation is only possible on the foundation of the capacity to make elementary distinctions and value judgments which are learned by studying the achievements and problems of the past of human civilization. The achievements of the past make value assessment possible.

How concepts of "past" and "progress" are being interpreted is dependent upon context. Artists, working at the beginning of the twenty-first century, might see a reflection of contemporary life experience in works of art that were made ages ago. If they find the ways of artistic thinking in the last century exhausted, they may see this as a good reason to look elsewhere for inspiration. When established forms of "contemporary art" have become a repetition of conventions and clichés—in short, a reactionary attitude, or worse, a serious decline—it is perfectly natural to inspect the achievements of artists of the past, from "before the fall" and learn from them. Nowadays many serious visual artists and composers look to a glorious past for examples, hoping to create an art which may help identify who we are, or who we want to be, and how we want to express and transcend ourselves.

In the reality in which Western civilization finds itself today, the modernist and postmodernist chimaeras of the last century are futile, unproductive, and irrelevant because they cannot contribute to solutions of problems that have surfaced quite recently and are so different in nature from the time which gave birth to modernism. As the twentieth century wanted to liberate itself from a "compromised" past to create the *Brave New World*, the twenty-first century opened up the sobering suspicion that much of that past could nonetheless be helpful in our present predicament. The fall of the Berlin Wall and the end of the Cold War, in combination with environmental problems and increasing globalization of trade and information technology, have changed the world in a profound way. Europe faces the challenge of reformulating its identity in relation to the world, which is also a cultural challenge; as far as new art is concerned, the lessons of the Renaissance could greatly help find an effective way through the maze of conflicting notions. Identity means awareness and understanding of the past, both on the collective and individual level. What defines the character of European civilization is its past cultural achievements and the best of the values they embody. This is the answer to the question of how to deal with them, how to interpret them and build upon them, in order to find the inner security and conviction that are the basis of all constructive action. In the twenty-first century, rebuilding culture—in its visual and musical forms—is a contemporary challenge with symbolic implications for the entire West. And to be able to prepare conditions for a cultural Renaissance, modernism, and its puerile progeny, has to be removed from its establishment position in the cultural field and its funding channeled toward the new art, which carries the creative fire needed to give to contemporary art the meaning and value it had before the onslaught of twentieth-century barbarism.

It is obvious that the attempts of modernist ideologies in the last century to "cancel the past" are not only silly, but in the present times, dangerous. For instance, to understand and reformulate European cultural identity, knowing and understanding the past is crucial: identity is the result of history. In Aldoux Huxley's celebrated novel *Brave New World* the authorities of a totalitarian state "cancelled" the past, knowing that an awareness of past experience would undermine the credibility and the power of the regime. Cancelling or rewriting the past, which is in fact the same thing, is the usual means of blotting out independent and, thus, subversive thinking in authoritarian societies like Nazi Germany, the Soviet Union, and North Korea. The attack upon the past is an attack upon civilization and thus, upon humanity. The inhuman nature of much modernist "music" (built upon a break with the past) is only the logical result of such an ideology.

The break with the past not only destroyed a living tradition, but also gave form to what now can be called the "museum culture." The distance between the present and the past seemed to turn artifacts and musical works from past periods into icons which came a long way from an inaccessible world, surrounded by a cult of veneration and commercial exploitation. In this museum culture, works of art (including musical works) are seen and listened to as objects in a case. In this way, their direct connection with real life seems to have vanished, their makers are treated like aliens from a different planet, with powers no longer attainable to modern man. There is a direct link between the exaggerated veneration of the masters of the past and the deeply felt inferiority complex of the artistic prowess of modern times. Without the nonsense of concept art and sonic art, the traditional museum collections and the traditional musical repertoire would not shine so brilliantly. The break with the past seemed to make a direct inner connection with an artistic practice impossible. Instead of history as a source of accessible and useful examples (as it was in premodern times), it became "a different country" and a cult. The attempts of new classical composers to recapture this "country" as something of ourselves is a courageous change of direction, with the aim of splintering the glass of the museum culture's glass cases, making a direct inner connection possible, and showing that the art of the past can be seen as something also living in the present. New classicism not only brings an old tradition to life again, but also makes a more direct emotional connection with the culture of the past possible as something not far removed in "another world." It shows the culture of the "museum" as something which also lives in the present. As there is no reason to consider the "museum culture" as something totally removed from our own time, or to see it as something negative in relation to contemporary art (it is not its own fault that a cult has been created around its products and that so much contemporary art is so bad), new classicism should be welcomed as a reassuring signal that, in the present, meaningful art also can be created. The whole idea of a museum culture as isolated from real life is being challenged by the current surge of mimetic art and music.

Meanwhile, there is a very good reason to support and cherish the islands of this so-called "museum culture," where the accumulation of knowledge and understanding of human life and civilization is expressed not in a purely scientific way but in the form of experiences which involve the entire human being and are thus accessible to anybody who takes the trouble to enter this territory and learns to understand its various artistic "languages." Fortunately, the reality is that the past still lives in the present, and if we want to maintain Western civilization and restore it according to its best ideas, we should be warned against utopias which cancel the humanistic and spiritual/expressive qualities of art. Purely materialistic and rationalistic philosophies of art inevitably carry in them the seeds of primitivism and barbarism. In these days, a classi-

cism which draws its understanding of civilization from the lessons of
the past seems to be the best possible way to counter utopianism and its
tendency to dehumanize society and the individual.

Is this "conservative"? The answer will be clear: no. It is progressive in
the sense that the Italian Renaissance was progressive, progressive in the
sense of making things better, trying to achieve a better artistic quality,
and by following superb examples of a glorious past. This notion of "better" is only possible in a world view where hierarchical thinking in connection with value and quality matters is taken for granted. However, in
a society as egalitarian as our Western one, where democratization has
also been understood as applicable to territories like the arts, this is often
considered as "elitist" and thus, un- or antidemocratic, an attitude which
cannot result otherwise than in an undermining of creative ambition and
marginalization of the best of talents. It is a sign of primitivism, of erosion, and not of social "progress." There is as much a link between the
aristocratic, "elitist" attitude toward the arts in Renaissance times (and
the ages directly following this glorious period) and the formidable quality of its art production, as there is between the modern democratic world
and the deplorable state of its art—that is, as exhibited in the official,
established public spaces and as supported by the state. The primitivism
of "official" contemporary art and contemporary music is a reflection of
the primitivism of the society which supports it—how could it be otherwise? On this point it may be enlightening to mention the anthropologist
Daniel Everett's memoirs of his thirty-year stay with a primitive tribe in
the Amazon jungle, the Pirahas (*Don't Sleep, There Are Snakes*, Profile
Books/Pantheon, 2008). This isolated community lives the way their fore-
bears lived for thousands of years, and they share a couple of remarkable
characteristics: they have a simple language and speak in short sentences;
they do not believe in gods, have no idea of spirituality, and do not
believe in an afterlife; they are not conscious of the past or the future but
live exclusively in the present; they have a strong resistance toward out-
siders which they dub "crooked heads"; they don't use numbers but
words for amounts like "a little" or "much," but nothing for ten, or five,
or one hundred; their society is like a commune: an egalitarian, nonhier-
archical social system which seems to be quite effective for them; they are
not interested in learning agriculture and are happy with their hunter/
gatherer existence; they have no interest in producing artwork. The remarkable thing is that they are, or strongly seem to be, a happy people
who see nothing wrong or "restricted" in their way of living and thus
want to keep things as they have always been: not surprisingly, they
resist modernization. They are traditionalists and conservatives in the
reactionnary, uncreative sense, clearly forced to remain as they are by the
strong limitations their natural environment brings upon them. Do these
characteristics not sound familiar? Are there not a number of people
living in the modern West with many of these characteristics (sometimes

even including the hunter/gatherer mentality), people for whom the total absence of culture and the territory of the mind and spirit is not experienced as an absence, but as a happy state of unconsciousness? One can find these tribes everywhere in the big cities of the West, in spite of the absence of limitations like those of the Amazon jungle environment. It must be said that, apparently, the Pirahas are perfectly adapted to their difficult life in primitive conditions where their lack of civilizational interests can be excused. But to find these typical primitive characteristics in the midst of a so-called civilized and wealthy world, is — to say the least — rather disturbing. It is not the primitive tribes in the jungles who need civilization, but many areas within civilized societies themselves, which, in their educational systems, often seem to fail to teach the basic tenets of what it means to live in a civilized world.

The artists and composers who dedicate themselves to the task of restoration of cultural traditions, including the civilizational values they embody, feel the need to contribute to the core of what the best of European civilization has been. The need for a restoration of European and Western culture and cultural identity in the broadest sense is felt everywhere, and the pioneers of this new classicism are the first artists who have rightly understood the challenge of renewal of the Western world in the twenty-first century, a renewal which gives the best of the past its due and sees it as a spring-board for a more civilized world and a more civilized contemporary creation. They deserve our attention and our support because they may find the themes and subjects that will symbolize the path taken by society as a whole.

SIX

The Search for Meaning

The American composer George Rochberg (1918–2005) began his career as a brilliant follower of post-1923 Schönberg with a spiky, tough twelve-tone music, which made him quite famous in American avant-garde circles in the 1950s and 1960s. In 1964, life dealt him a devastating blow: his teenage son died of a brain tumor. This experience forced him to rethink his artistic project and he concluded that "music" which was "objective," in fact: the entire then-modern serialist project was misconceived and incapable of creating meaning in human terms, of relating to those realities of human life that really matter. He turned toward the past in a search for a musical style with the expressive means that could give voice to universal human life experience, and he found these in Beethoven's late quartets and in Mahler's symphonies. Being an accomplished modernist, it cost him several years of hard work to "unlearn" his acquired composition habits and to delve deeply into the tonal territory, to find out how tonality worked effectively in these marvels of expressive music, which he took as his examples. Yet, his new-classical works do not entirely convince. Either they are too close to their examples, rather bland and without their free invention, or—where old-fashioned style elements are combined with twentieth-century sounds—just not composed well enough. But the point is that Rochberg discovered an important truth: music is a humanist art form, and thus mimetic and communicative. His courage to reject modernist ideology in a time when this was considered *de rigeur* deserves the greatest respect; in spite of an enormous amount of negative critique, he stuck to his new principles. Another American composer, Peter Lieberson (1946–2011), struggled through a comparable trajectory. Beginning as a very capable modernist, he changed the language of his work drastically in the late 1990s, when he fell in love with the brilliant mezzo soprano, Lorraine Hunt, whom he married in 1999. Tragically, she died in 2006 of cancer, after which Lieberson himself was diagnosed with the same illness. Lieberson's "Neruda Songs" of 2005 show his uninhibited turn toward a traditional, lyrical language where echoes from Schönberg and Berg mingle with a colorful French subtlety and harmonic sensitivity. The tools he found in styles of the past enabled him to give his music a strongly expressive quality, and these love songs radiate an authentic inspiration, in a tender, pastel-like atmosphere. Both Rochberg and Lieberson were really talented composers and thus they saw through the restrictions of modernism at the moment they were touched by life experiences which challenged the meaning of their artistic project. And they both turned toward the past for solutions, for the obvious reason that an art form which had been developed and refined over the ages, which embodied artistic and spiritual understanding as cumulated over an immense time span, is richer in human and artistic experience than the invention of "objective sound," where structuring the sonic surface is all there is to achieve. This may be nice for a while, but in the case of a really musical composer, there will come a moment when his real nature longs to break through the limitations of his own time and reach a universal artistic level. The tragedy of the twentieth century is that instead of opening up wide horizons of possibilities (as modernist ideologies have always claimed), the developments of new music created a mental prison of ideologies that could not but stifle the natural drives of real musical talents. The aforementioned composers are perfect examples of what happens when a culture throws away its past, but also how individual independence can liberate the spirit from the conformism of the "professional world." In these touching examples, it was the past which opened up a future, and in Lieberman's case, resulted in at least one authentic, truly beautiful piece.

Later generations of composers similarly fed up with atonal modernism, and without needing life catastrophe to turn away from stuffy orthodoxies, either joined the blandness of processed music kitsch, tapped the folklore of non-Western cultures, or wasted themselves in the quasi-philosophical territory of concept music (à la John Cage, who "created" the musical equivalent of Marcel Duchamp's urinal: the "piece" consisting of silence with the title *4 Minutes and 33 Seconds*) and left musical territory altogether. It shows that the cultural past still was an imposing presence, intimidating for the small talents and positively lethal for the talentless, who thus clung fanatically to the modernist timeline in the hope of achieving some recognition in academic circles. The past had become an inaccessible bastion of superb achievement, the mental climate of which seemed out of reach, except for really gifted, independent individuals like Lieberson, or the French composer Nicolas Bacri. The past had become "another planet" and its meaning something to be doubted or denied.

But is it possible that the art of the past loses its meaning just because it is old, simply as a result of the passing of time and the many changes in society? As a result of more recent periods coming in between older ones, influencing our perception? Would our historical awareness not be the very thing that distorts our perception of true artistic content of past cultural periods? We visit museums to see artistic masterpieces. We go to concerts and listen to great works of dead composers. But do we *really* understand what we see, what we hear? To what extent is our vision and hearing *corrupted* by more recent layers of experience and our interpretation of history, or by a cultural erosion which would only become visible—with hindsight—during a regeneration? Has our aesthetic appreciation been informed and enriched, or blunted by more recent experiences? Are we, in fact, like medieval Italians, walking around Roman ruins without really understanding what they are, yet still impressed by their grandeur and beauty? The challenge for artists in the twenty-first century is to find a way back to the reality of artistic experience, to the "innocence" of natural human creativity, and not be distracted by the cynical triviality of modern life and the erosion of culture which can be seen all around us. New classical composers work from the conviction that the basis of art music has to be restored, that its original sources have to be rediscovered, and that the best context for such endeavor is the notion of tradition, *not* as an academic, codified body of rules, but as a dynamic process of discovery, interpretation, and free individual variation. New, original territory can be found in the personal variations created by individual artists using existing materials with distinct vocabularies, and not necessarily in the exploration of new materials. It is in what is *done* with the materials where music is to be found, *not* in the materials themselves.

The re-creation of a lost artistic tradition can be an isolated, individual project, but understanding of such a project is greatly helped within the context of some broader cultural framework. Over the last years, signals of such a framework have begun to emerge. First, the European Union is aspiring to its own cultural identity, albeit still only vaguely supposed. The necessity to define what Europe really is has gained momentum since the fall of the Berlin Wall in 1989 and the subsequent opening up of Eastern Europe. This debate is fraught with the ethical problems of Europe's history, which has brought us the sublime and the evil in almost equal measure. Which part will form European self-understanding, crime or creation? Second, the awareness that civilization is unthinkable without concern for the natural environment, which is itself fundamentally cyclical and "traditional" and cannot be subjected to manipulation without the serious danger of upsetting the delicate balance of natural systems; this increasing importance of the environmental problem in public debate reflects the need for a redefinition of priorities in our society, especially where progressing technological means threaten to absorb more and more natural resources. A renewed interest in spirituality is a third point of orientation. Spirituality is a natural aspect of human experience and indeed the basis of all civilization, either expressed through involvement in traditional religion, in the many new, freer forms of spiritual dedication, or in a secularity shaped by humanism (which itself could be considered a result of spirituality). The emancipation of the individual from the overbearing authority and worldly power of traditional religion has been one of the great achievements of Europe and the opportunities opened up by Enlightenment values prove a beacon for emancipation all over the world—but that does not mean that the religious spirit has disappeared: it has spread to other territories like art (and sometimes even science), showing that the human being needs inspiration which comes from beyond the material chains of cause and effect.

And last but not least, the influx of immigrants from non-European cultures, many of them Muslim countries, have formed communities that often have difficulty integrating into European society, partly due to discrimination from the side of the Europeans, partly as a result of the nature of Muslim cultures, which, at some fundamental points, differ from Western values. To integrate into another culture, the host culture should have values that are attractive and invite adaptation, and with the term "values" is meant something more than material advantages. But since European civilization has undergone a transition from its own cultural traditions into what could be called "the modern world," what Muslim immigrants often find amidst a material wealth and a relatively well-organized society is a frightening absence of civilized values, an indifference to notions that give meaning to life and to spiritual perspectives, a rampant, egoistic materialism combined with populist vulgarity, a public space besmeared by the lowest common denominator, where there no longer seems to be an awareness of the distinctions between superior and inferior, of important and unimportant, of private and public space, reflecting a general malaise of value, a nihilism parading as freedom, tolerance, and cultural relativism. To many immigrants, European society as a whole—that is, as experienced in public space—is banal, empty, egoistic, and under the surface: *primitive.* (Let us not forget that in developing countries where public space is physically dangerous, it is the local, *old* culture which keeps society more or less intact, often fully independently from the authorities of the state.) Why would one want to adapt to a culture that no longer believes in itself and its achievements, that often ignores its best values, its achievements from the past, its highest aspirations? It would be disastrous if some form of European, positive cultural self-respect and aspiration would exclusively become the instrument of fundamentalist right-wing political movements, using it as a weapon to "defend" Europe against "hostile" immigration; it should be a concern for everybody who understands the cultural crisis in which Europe finds itself.

The Europeanization of Muslim immigrants can only work if there is something positive to integrate into, if Europe no longer exclusively highlights the crimes of its past but rediscovers all the greatness that reflects its creative spirit, a spirit that is perfectly capable of absorbing "foreign" elements without destroying them. It is possible for a European Muslim to preserve some important identity-building elements of his homeland and yet become fully European, like so many Jews who—after acquiring civil rights at the beginning of the nineteenth century—became part of Europe's leading cultural elite. (The abysmal injustice and crime that happened to them in the twentieth century should be a profound lesson about processes of assimilation.) One of the central values of European civilization is the idea that one can be European *by choice*, independent from descent, class, or religious adherence and thus belong to a community which is held together by civilizational values instead of by more primitive bonds like clans, tribes, and power elites. Europe's humanist and cultural traditions, including universal values and hence related to the best in non-European cultures, are something to cherish, not to condemn or to suppress in an act of self-destruction, nor to love unconditionally and uncritically. Acknowledging the greatness of European civilization does not mean that its aberrations and crimes are denied or excused; feeling committed to one's culture does not automatically mean "chauvinism." It is in this territory that art, and especially new art, can act as a metaphor for cultural renewal in the broadest sense.

The greatest enemy of a positive and constructive Western or European cultural self-image is the idea of cultural relativism. In his groundbreaking book, *The Defeat of the Mind* (1987), the French philosopher Alain Finkielkraut analyses the sources of cultural relativism that led to the trendy multicultural political-correctness to which the current right wing populist revival in Europe is the sad and primitive reaction. It is rewarding to go somewhat deeper into this subject, because it relates to the theme of this book on a profound level. Cultural relativism claims that every culture has its own merits and cannot be measured against some cultural quality standard *outside* existing cultures. Western and European culture is a culture like any other, and when we evaluate other cultures, we simply act in an imperialist way, spreading our network of prejudices—which are rooted in our local history and local culture—over the reality of another culture, thereby missing its innate character. In this view, individuals are before anything else members of and expressions of the group; the tribe. They are locked up in the cultural tradition in which they find themselves. This is then also projected upon the relationship between Western/European culture and the other cultures which were colonized in the nineteenth century: members of non-European traditions supposedly form a monolithic mass dominated by the overwhelming character of their culture. Their individuality is submerged in the collective, which is the local culture that had been "poisoned" by Western imperialist thought and action. For that reason, to avoid chauvinism and imperialism, the "other" from another culture has to be fully respected in his or her own, foreign customs, habits, convictions, religious rites; all our talk about universal values and human rights are just the product of *our* local traditional culture, with the result that we have no "right" to criticize non-European convictions and customs. Of course this is the result of the awareness of (1) European capacities of barbarism, as shown in the last century, which invoke inferiority feelings and (2) guilt over colonialization, which uprooted local cultures in the eastern and southern regions of the globe. This cultural relativism, which can be projected upon any form of culture (in the widest sense) is an easy escape from a deeper Western problem: that of the notion of "universal civilizational values."

The idea that there are no universal values of civilization against which cultures and traditions (including of the West) can be measured goes back to the eighteenth-century German philosopher Johann Gottfried Herder, who mounted an attack upon Enlightenment values of truth, beauty, and the good. He claimed that every epoch and every culture has its own version of "reason," concluding that the individual is before anything else rooted in his own local tradition, what he calls the "Volksgeist," throwing the individual back into tribal identity and to the detriment of his personal, individual identity. Cultivated in nineteenth-century Germany, which strived after unification following a long period of fragmented backwardness, this idea formed the fertile humus for chauvinistic nationalism and, a century later, fascism. The reason for this critique upon the Enlightenment is the element of dryness embedded in its rationalism and the experience of existential uprootedness, which is the inevitable result of the emancipation of the individual from a world in which feudal hierarchies and the power of organized religion kept society firm in place, offering a strong emotional experience of belonging. But, of course, emancipation of the individual does not mean that everything of traditional, pre-modern society was destructive, bad for the people who were born in it. In an ideal world, the structures of society considered as a dynamic framework ask responsibility from the partaking individuals, who *in freedom* accept their responsibility on civilizational and ethical grounds. This implies that first, the individual has to develop from being embedded within a group toward a veritable freedom of thought, which is always (also in an ideal world) a trajectory from a situation with transparent ego boundaries toward one in which ego boundaries are firmly established, even if also functioning within a group. Free individualism can still function productively upon the older structures of a traditional society. Enlightenment values are a big improvement in terms of civilization, as far as they do not destroy older values compatible with them: from an emancipated point of view, older notions can be translated, transformed into the new situation. So, to some extent Herder had a point: if Enlightenment values would mean giving up one's sense of belonging to a place, to a people and its history—in short, factors of importance because of their emotional relatedness, the new freedom would lose much of its meaning because there is not much meaning to be found in a freedom spent in unhappiness, depression, alienation, and nihilism. But by claiming the importance of the "tribe" over the individual, he closed the pathway to the possibility that the individual can overcome the restrictions of the "tribe" and his own historically determined cultural climate to reach a higher awareness, where he or she can find universal civilizational values that are, in every developed culture, compatible in their essentials.

Finkielkraut relates the story of Johann Wolfgang von Goethe, the great German poet, author, and cultural philosopher (1749–1832), who read an old Chinese novel and discovered striking similarities with his own epos in rime, *Hermann und Dorothea*. In spite of all the differences, both works touched upon universal human experience. Goethe's conclusion was that even while people are rooted in their locality and their culture, and anchored in their place and period, they could still overcome the limitations of their situation and meet and understand the universally human in works of art from other cultures and other times.

The idea of cultural relativity in relation to non-Western cultures had, on the wave of the general emancipation movements and, after 1945, the deep disillusionment about European civilization, an unexpected effect *within* Western culture: if Western cultural traditions cannot claim superiority in a global context, making value distinctions within our society would be meaningless as well. Together with the trend of an increasingly misunderstood "democratization" of the individual citizen, hierarchical value frameworks became increasingly suspect, were related to suppression, domination, and the exclusion of the uninitiated, with the result that—for many people—the context of the different phenomena of life disappeared. So, your taste is as good as mine, and there is no difference in value between pop music, classical music, film music, rap, pictures in museums, advertisements, Shakespeare, sitcoms, graffiti, needlework in old people's homes, Boulez, fashion, cooking, mating, classical architecture, digestion, and so on. Thinking along this line inevitably results in the general feeling that *nothing* matters, that nothing has any meaning. When everything is as meaningful as any other thing, meaning has disappeared. (A good example is the Dutch new music financing system: *anything* can be "good enough" to deserve to be paid for.)

Obviously this form of "freedom," of "emancipation" and "democratization" is emptying life experience of any chance for development, achievement, personal growth, and especially of culture and art. Any development to something better, in any field, is only possible if there is an idea that there is indeed something better. This is not progressiveness, but merely the operation of quality standards. If, in the arts, the idea of quality hierarchy is abandoned altogether, then the masterpieces of art, from the past as well as from the present (if there are any), become isolated islands without a framework with which they can become understandable and meaningful. In this way, cultural relativism is destructive not only in the context of private life, but especially for public life, because normative standards lose ground, they become entirely arbitrary. In this way, civilization is being broken down from the inside, being deleted of all the instruments for development and comparative evaluation that cultural traditions, with their in-built quality standards, so evidently offered. Only when life experience is treated hierarchically, in terms of meaning and significance, can it become understandable and can truth and meaning be found. As the old Chinese religious/spiritual book, the *I Ching* says: everything of the human body is important and has its significance, but the parts are not equally important.

Next to the development of cultural relativism, another strong source of chest beating European self-deprecation must be mentioned: the critical examination of European history after 1945 by the intellectual and artistic elite, justifying their dislike of the European past by highlighting the bloody wars, colonial crimes, political disasters, and the like, as if this were the *only* thing European civilization had produced—a grotesque exaggeration, excusable because of the two world wars, but after half a century, a petrified cliché. The "demise" of the *grand récits*, the "great stories" of mankind, is a typical example of this kind of exaggeration, as if *all* "great ideas" must inevitably be evil ideologies. The mental malaise in Europe, fearful of losing its empty wealth and security, has thus been fed by a combination of different reactions to the wars, decolonization, rapid industrialization, and the realization that it is no longer a real political power in the global context. The erosion of religion in combination with an increasingly capitalist materialism robs the human being of any possible faith in ideas that may transcend his individual life, ideas that could thus give his life a meaning and provide the energy to improve those things that need to be improved. Deep down, every human being (apart from the Brazilian Pirahas) longs to be part of something bigger than himself, which stimulates personal growth and spiritual development. The instinct to transcend, to achieve great things, is a typically human one, which can inspire both grand disasters and great achievements in culture and science, an instinct which—it could be argued—is a universal trait of the human species and which lies at the heart of all the great cultures the world has seen. And this instinct begins with the capacity to make distinctions in terms of value and quality.

The capacity for making meaningful distinctions is typical of the species, as the creation of art is, which can only exist on the condition of this capacity. Cultural relativity is incompatible with the existence of art; it isolates the individual from the deepest layers of his being. The often misunderstood psychologist Carl Gustav Jung (1875–1961) suggested that humanity in general possesses a deep layer of common life experience, which is the accumulated experience of the species and inherited automatically down the generations, which he called the *collective subconscious*. Metaphorically speaking, this is like a layer of instinctive notions underneath the individual, personal subconscious. From this deepest layer emerges the emotionally loaded imagery that populates myths, religions, and spiritual dreams, carrying symbols of emotional experience, remaining valid over time in spite of changes on the surface of life. This collective subconscious may be the ground in which the individual roots find their creative and spiritual "food," without which the "tree" of civilization would not have any stability and continuity. Where the Enlightenment values elevate and emancipate the individual above the collective, the artist can—from a liberated position—look back upon tradition and the past, which are no longer symbols of suppression and domination, and transform tradition from a dominating force into a supportive one. This elevated position makes it possible to reach a more or less objective freedom and universalism, from which qualitative hierarchies become visible and make possible the evaluation of one's own culture, as well as the cultures from other areas and periods. This is something very different from "chauvinism" or "imperialist thought" because one's own culture is subjected to the same scrutiny. It is the opposite of superficial cultural relativism, and is a workable solution to the problem of overabundance of information about other than Western cultures. While awareness of value in other cultures, acquired through the accessibility of information, is kept intact, the values of one's own culture share the same critical and/or loving look, which makes possible value judgment for creative purposes and the "rooting" in a traditional culture which serves the individual artist best. This is the position of the new-classical composer: handling quality hierarchies without the need to hark back to a position of superiority complexes which were the result of ignorance. This position makes it also possible to rightly judge phenomena like pop music, media "culture," Chinese opera, Congo drumming, and country and western ballads as freely as we can judge Aztec architecture, pre-Islamic pottery, and Ural folk dancing without Western prejudices coming in the way. We don't need to condemn inferior art to be able to prefer the best wherever we find it, and what could be against finding and making use of the riches on which we are sitting? If new-classical composers revive aesthetic and expressive values of past traditions, they do this from a position which could only arise after the entire trajectory of modernism (and the defeat of thinking and of artistry as represented by postmodernism), have run their course. In the end, the beauties and sublime qualities of the best of the European cultural tradition become visible again without the stain of chauvinism or reactionary tribal instinct celebration. The concept of tradition becomes possible again as a dynamic civilizational force, which can be practised in freedom.

So, there are good reasons why artists would revive European cultural traditions and why the art world and the music world should welcome this thaw in the relations between artists and public. This rapprochement does not mean a lowering of standards on the side of the artists, but an acknowledgment that both parties share a common ground. And this ground is the inheritance of past cultural experience. The keyword here is *roots*. People can only be creative and constructive if they have roots, if there is a minimum of psychological and emotional continuity and stability, provided by experiences, which have proved meaningful and workable. And it will also be clear that by "roots" is *not* meant a narrow-minded nationalism and xenophobia, or worse, the "Blut und Boden" mentality which created such havoc in the last century, but rather the acceptance and emotional embracing of a civilizational perspective which reaches far into the past, a perspective open to all participants with enough sensitivity and imagination to be able to explore its riches. A modern society which has no roots in the past, which lacks a framework and the necessary experience for making value judgments, is prone to disintegration, whatever its present achievements. The West needs to use its accumulation of human experience as the basis of its understanding of itself and the world, exposing the bad but also the good and fruitful, and allowing again the idealism without which no great deeds on whatever level are possible.

How does the classical tradition (in music) embody the values of Europe's humanistic tradition? Because music is nonconceptual, this cannot unambiguously be pinned down: as language is the "what" of things, music is the "how." Music explores the "how" of man's inner, emotional life in a way that makes "resonance" and identification possible. It brings the contents of individual experience into consciousness through an aesthetic stylization which gives them structure and beauty, and thus ennobles them, spiritualizes them, educating the emotional and reflective capacities of the listener if he is receptive to this process. This explains the strange phenomenon of musical experiences that are in themselves not very positive or agreeable, like the sombre and rather nihilistic *Second Piano Sonata* of Chopin, but yet can turn out to have an uplifting and "purifying" effect. In the darker corners of life we are not alone, we are understood down to the subtlest nuances, and we feel that even there a spiritual meaning can be experienced even if we cannot derive some clearly positive conclusion from it. The meaning of our lives, to which superb music is hinting, lies beyond our temporal understanding, bound as this understanding is to our physical, temporal world. In this way, music gives meaning to our inner life, whatever the nature of our experience, and tells us that—in spite of everything—our lives are *meaningful*, without the necessity of our conscious understanding. The miracle of life is greater and its strange mystery deeper than words can express adequately. At this point, music connects with religion, which also is supposed to spiritualize our life through rituals, myths, legends, and symbolic acts, whose ultimate meaning is deeper than their surface level. Of course, all this could just be a sophisticated self-delusion to take out the sting of our mortality, but given the rich fruits of a spiritualized life view, it seems better to take the risk that spirituality refers to something real and true, than to embrace the opposite position—and find out in due course that one has unnecessarily told oneself a nihilistic and depressing story, thereby denying oneself a potent source of life-enhancing energy. The presence of the Divine—if such a thing exists—can be experienced through this process of spiritualization, of an awakening to the awareness that we are much more than a bag of neurons steering our body. It is for this reason that music is "the language of the soul," and the European musical tradition a cultivating agent of the life experiences of the free and responsible individual.

The classical tradition, reaching back to its earliest beginnings in the Middle Ages, covers a wide territory of human experience, from cosmic reflection (Palestrina, Bach, Pärt) to existential panic and despair (Mahler, middle Schönberg); from intimate happiness (Mozart, Brahms, Debussy) to tragic loneliness (Mozart, Brahms, Debussy); from heroic and transcendental faith (Beethoven) to heroic and stoic nihilism (Shostakovich). The other reason—in addition to the superb artistic quality of his work—that Beethoven is so important for the classical tradition is the remarkable fact that his music, on one hand, beautifully expresses subjective individuality and, on the other hand, so eloquently preaches the core values of civil society, values mainly developed from the Enlightenment onward: freedom, democracy, justice, individual development, ethical acuteness, community spirit, and the hope on a better future (which is something else from *artistic* utopianism). Music does not have "a message" but reflects our inner life in all its shades and spiritualizes it—thus confirming our spiritual existence. Even a powerfully primitive work like Stravinsky's *Sacre du Printemps*, which borders on the edge of what we can consider music, teaches us something about long-forgotten existential drives and fears that are still present in the deepest corners of our archaic collective memories, and even achieves an ennobling effect of the most primitive impulses (interestingly, the aesthetic process gets less convincing toward the end, where the orchestra is "flattened" into spasms of rhythm in the *Danse Sacrale*). Like Schönberg's *Fünf Orchesterstücke*, this fragile balance at the edge of the abyss cannot be repeated, as Stravinsky himself realized, and as the vain imitations of both pieces by other composers have shown. At the heart of the classical tradition lies the image of the human being as a sensitive individual, with an active inner emotional life, where his ideals, failings, moods, hopes, and fears are projected outward and shared. The development of this tradition seems to suggest that the goal is to reach the autonomy and full blossoming of the individual, while relating him again and again to the forces that determine his exis-

tence and to the society in which he finds himself. It is utterly individual-
istic and at the same time, collective; both reaching to the stars and dig-
ging into the earth, capable of communicating the eternal as well as the
temporal, the objective as well as the subjective, but always addressing
the individual human being as the center of awareness and illuminating
his inner life, telling him about his experiences, or about what he would
be capable of experiencing. In this sense, classical music is a truly
transcending art and at the same time, truly human. This combination of
transcendence and humanity found its first expression in classical
Greece, shaping the core of European cultural and psychological identity
and propelling it into ever-developing forms and variations.

As there is a hierarchy in the qualities of interior experience, there is
also a hierarchy in the qualities of classical music relating to them. Therefore, music of which the type of expression is rather naive, like much of
Tchaikovsky and Rachmaninoff, or Dvorak and Mendelssohn, can still
have an ennobling effect upon the listener who is on its wavelength;
although still authentic and "honest," it would as yet be an invitation to
climb up the ladder of musical sophistication and try richer experiences.
Not everybody needs to enjoy the sublime, which is accessible through a
trajectory of education of the senses. As long as we know it is out there,
the prospect of such a possible experience offers us a worthwhile goal in
our spiritual development.

The various stages of the development of European civilization find
expression in its musical tradition, which finds ever new emotional territory to be aestheticized and ever new ideals and aspirations to strive
after. This does not mean that composers themselves are always aware of
this process, as shown by the examples of Wagner and Scriabine, who
wed confused ideas to music deserving better purposes. Also, it should
not be assumed that people professing to "understand" and "love" classical music would necessarily follow up its implications, as the stories of
art-loving concentration camp brutes demonstrate. To project crimes like
this, or even the Holocaust, back into the very fabric and character of
Europe's *cultural*, *artistic* tradition, as is shown by modernist ideologies
and—as an example from cultural philosophy—in George Steiner's *In
Bluebeard's Castle*, is in itself a kind of crime: it is an attempt to philosophically kill off what two world wars have not quite been able to destroy.
Steiner's book is thus in line with the dehumanizing attempts of modernism in the last century to get rid of the last vestiges of beauty and spiritual nobility that had been left after the catastrophe. It will be clear that
recapturing something of this tradition is not a luxury, but a necessity,
directly related to the survival of European/Western civilization as a
whole.

At this point, it may be necessary to counter the modernist argument
that the Holocaust showed humanity's *real nature*, that it is merely an
apotheosis of built-in evil of human nature, and that human civilization

as a whole reached its true historical pinnacle—its bloody *telos*—in Hitler. In other words: human nature is Hitler nature. In combination with the religious denouement that obviously there is no protecting, well-meaning, intervening anthropomorphic God to help the victims of murderous horror, any attempt to have a positive opinion about human civilization after the Second World War seemed preposterous and an insult to the numerous graves, persistent witnesses to remind us of the possibility of immense human failure. As it is obvious that, if there is a God, "it" must be something rather different from the concept as taught by the Christian, Jewish, and Islamic religious traditions (i.e., in the literal descriptions in naïve images), it will be clear that sweeping generalizations like "human nature" and "civilization," as directly related to grand-scale crime, misrepresent the reality of human distinction. The majority of people are, by nature, not inclined to crime and murder, as a small minority clearly is (depending on circumstance and chance). The catastrophe of Nazism resulted from an "elite" of primitive cranks, of people lacking essential awareness of civilization, getting into power because of particular historical circumstances. That many of them carried some veneer of educational sophistication—going to classical music concerts, loving Renaissance painting—does not mean that the music they listened to, the paintings they viewed, caused the evil they committed in their field of operation. It should be clear that human civilization is an ongoing attempt to master primitive impulses, to educate the inner life, to develop the senses, to harmonize and order society, and that art is an important instrument to that end. When art does not appear to be able to stop evil from happening, it is the human being to be blamed, not art. The two world wars have long roots in history, but it was the still primitive side of man surfacing. The wars were the result of parts of European populations being not civilized *enough*, instead of simply the result of Europe's civilization. As far as primitive rumblings threaten to destabilize society, this shows that European/Western civilization is not finished and still has a long way to go to achieve some level of sophistication comparable to the best artistic endeavors of its past. To halt at the nihilism of Holocaust and modernism as if they were final points of history beyond which there is no way to go, is a suicidal delusion. Europe survived its worst catastrophe thus far and should recapture its real creative and constructive spirit, which can be experienced in the great works of its musical tradition: there, one can hear how a spirit of transcendental meaning orders all kinds of emotional impulses, ennobles them, refines them, and brings harmony to what otherwise would be a chaotic collection of confusing instincts.

The country that suffered the most from the postwar modernist revolution was Germany. Its musical tradition was considered contaminated by the annexation of the Nazis, and romanticism especially was seen as a pool of evil and bad taste. Wagner, the former icon of "Aryan" culture and its anti-Semitism, became the symbol of everything that was wrong with tonality, expression, and the so-called "humanist tradition" in music. Postwar new music had to symbolize the birth of a new Germany, a country fully integrated into Western democracy and joining Western modernity, of which the United States was the leader. In music, modernism became the flagship of German modernity, but a flagship that had left its original harbor for a sea where audiences did not want to follow. While new modernist music was supported and funded by the institutions, the central performance culture was restored as a museum culture, where the "dangerous" masterpieces of the past could be enjoyed as objects behind the glass of history, and thus reasonably "safe." The Bayreuth Festival with its famous theater, set up by Wagner for his operas, where they could be performed in the best theatrical and acoustical conditions, was cleansed after the war by his grandsons who introduced a thoroughly "sobered" presentation which focused upon the timeless aspects of this impressive oeuvre. With the German culture of the past safely locked up in the museum, its present incarnation, modernism, showed its negation, which carried the symbolism of safety as well: atonal, modernist Germans were good Germans, however ugly, barbaric, and nihilistic the results.

The story of the composer Walter Braunfels is typical. He was a young and gifted composer in the 1920s, one who stuck to the German romantic tradition, in a fierce rejection of both Schönbergian atonalism and the current hard-edged neoclassicism, with its associations with popular music. He got quite some success with his operas and was even approached by the upcoming Nazi party to write something for them, an invitation which Braunfels rejected out of hand. During the 1930s, he was marginalized and lost his job at the Cologne conservatory for being a "half-Jew," and his music disappeared out of sight. After the war, he tried to make a career for the second time, in the conviction that his stainless past would give him the opportunity to escape the taboo upon tradition. But then, he did not fit the cultural identity that the country had created for itself, and he saw his chances evaporate. Only recently has his opera "Die Vögel" been rediscovered and staged, in Germany as well as in the United States. It appeared to be a good work, enjoying deserved success. In fact, his music—which is a kind of "soft Richard Strauss," sympathetic and well-made—has been suppressed twice by totalitarianism: first by the Nazis, then by the German "avant-garde" who found that this music was not *zeitgemäss*, not of the present time.

The German cultural tradition offers a wide variety of different strands, and its premodern musical tradition is a gift to the world and to Europe; the best of this tradition is not just German, but European through and through and thus open to reinterpretation, as any cultural tradition is. In Germany, however, this may feel like a dangerous arrogance and chauvinism—an exaggerated fear resulting from guilt over the past. The works of great artists may be rooted in their national culture, but their greatness transcends it: great art is universal by nature. But in present-day Germany, its cultural heritage is felt as being exclusively *national*, and thus the shadow of national guilt and remorse falls over it. German musical culture thus presents a most odd picture: it sits on an incomparable historical richness, but its contemporary composers repeat and repeat the postwar dictum of guilt obligation, creating a sort of symbolical confirmation of the *untergang* of their musical culture, which otherwise is widely celebrated in a museum culture of the highest standards, especially in Germany itself. Modern music is accepted as the expression of a modern, liberal, Westernized Germany, and the almost insane contrast with its musical past is accepted as "normal"; attempts at revivalism, as can be seen in the Anglo-Saxon (David Matthews, John Corigliano) or French world (Nicolas Bacri, Richard Dubugnon,) seem, for the time being, too sensitive for Germany. As long as "modern music" in Germany strains under the taboo of the "dark period," its new music is imprisoned within the walls of a moralistic totalitarianism not much less suffocating than the communist cultural climate in the former Soviet Union. As Alex Ross brilliantly formulates in his *The Rest Is Noise*, "The great German tradition, with all its grandeurs and sorrows, is cordoned off, like a crime scene under investigation."

No doubt, now Germany has found itself, to its own great surprise, as the economic and political heart of Europe, younger generations will eventually feel a normal inclination to delve into the achievements of their past and be capable of handling it in a more objective way—and possibly new generations of composers will discover that they are the inheritors of an overwhelmingly rich source of inspiration and beauty and not merely of war catastrophe and Hitler's taste, to which atonality was a neurotic defense mechanism. Given the intensity of musical talent available in this tortured nation, it is to be expected that at some stage they will get enough of their *Nachkriegschuldbewältigungsmusik* and move on to more constructive perspectives. In cultural terms, atonal modernism is a "German" invention, dialectically opposed to the philosophical and expressive tenets of classicism; if the postwar political rebirth of Germany can be considered a rebirth, metaphorically, of the humanist and classical Germany of the late eighteenth century (with its godfathers Goethe and Schiller), it is to be expected that a return to these original sources of timeless inspiration and humanism in terms of music will at some stage break through the hard scale of self-imposed, outworn restrictions. After all, the riches of tonality found in the German-speaking world their greatest realizations.

Understanding the European classical tradition in music means understanding European/Western civilization from the inside. But what is the legacy of the body of modernist art within this context? In the course of time, modernism loses its more ephemeral aspects like "historical significance" and "revolutionary qualities," and is judged increasingly upon its potential universal merits: its artistic qualities, its power to move, to create meaning, to enrich our lives. It is legitimate to respect Picasso's *Demoiselles d'Avignon* for its revolutionary nature in the context of its own time, while also acknowledging that it is an aesthetically inferior painting. His *Guernica* or the works from his pink and blue periods, on the other hand, have more to offer in terms of expression and aesthetic quality. The *Demoiselles* is only intelligible in the context of the supposedly "suffocating bourgeois taste" against which it was a subversive scream; a scream from the suppressed jungle of instincts, like the novels of D. H. Lawrence and Henry Miller, who both, in their revolutionary enthusiasm, forgot that there are some type of instincts which indeed are better suppressed to make civilization possible. They and figures like Freud, Picasso, Schönberg, and the early Stravinsky were reacting against the negative aspects of the European cultural climate in the nineteenth century but not against the idea of European culture as a whole. It is likely that the legacy of modernism will be historical rather than aesthetic and artistic: a reaction against ghosts which have meanwhile disappeared.

When modernism is left behind as an outdated thought experiment and European art finds again its own roots and artistic aspirations, the concepts of "traditional," "conservative," and "modern" will obtain a new meaning which will be different from that of the last century. These labels are psychological constructs over a reality which is related to different contexts. In the musical world of the twenty-first century, sonic art is "conservative" and new tonal music "modern," a new form of tradition and of "classical music." "Tradition" now means a dynamic mentality based upon the foundation of experience of the past, not a reactionary attitude that wants to keep things as they were in an attempt to freeze a situation that came into being in another context (as current remnants of modernism are). A living tradition is based upon the principle of *imitation*: what has proven to work well is imitated and, in the hands of artists with an individual personality, this "imitation" gradually acquires, after their period of apprentice, the stamp of originality. Originality is a psychological quality, a personality trait, and can never be a conscious intention. The very few pupils Maurice Ravel accepted had to work according to this principle: they had to closely imitate carefully chosen examples and if they felt they had to deviate from them, it was—as Ravel said—in the deviation that their originality showed itself. It is a learning process in which respect for, and love and understanding of, the achievements of older generations stimulate new creation, with originality not as a goal but as a welcome byproduct.

How would this learning process be reflected in education? In pre-nineteenth century times, the learning trajectory of artists consisted of studying with a master, which meant imitating him as much as possible, and later on, going your own way. Successful artists like Rubens and

Rembrandt ran a studio with assistants, who were aspirant artists, who carried out menial jobs like preparing the materials, preparing the canvasses, and painting parts of them under the instructions of the master and closely watching as he brought the process to an end. It was a learning process in which academic theorizing and standardization had no place. It was first and foremost a *practical* and *hierarchical* one. From the aspirant artist, it required modesty, respect, and loving dedication to the art form, which provided the basis of his own later artistic confidence. It was an instinctive, intuitive, and spiritual process which cannot be institutionalized, because regulations, rules, dogmas, and orthodoxies, in the attempt to standardize the learning process, tend to petrify something that is by its nature fluid, practical but also irrational, and deeply rooted in temperament and individuality.

Institutionalization of the artistic learning process means casting a rationalistic substructure over a natural phenomenon, which is in itself understandable because of the enlargement of scale; for classes to be organized, time schedules have to be set up, salaries settled, materials managed, and so forth. Big scale requires standardization, as we can see all around us, and standardization tends to stamp out individual creativity. Someone like J. S. Bach did not have to study at an institution to fully develop his capabilities, just as Mozart had the luck of private tuition from his erudite father and countless travel experiences. But French painting in the seventeenth century as monitored by the *académie*—one of the first institutions set up by a government for the specific purpose of furthering national art—began to suffer from "academism," inaugurating the split between individual creativity and "official traditional instruction," leading in the nineteenth century (under the influence of the then developing scientific paradigm) to the codification of the visual arts and music in the academies and conservatories.

Almost all great composers since Beethoven either had no academic training, or in case they let themselves be subjected to it, strongly rebelled against its life-draining character, or/and got into trouble with "official authority." It has to be stressed that this specific kind of rebellion against authority was not common in the old master–pupil system, because in those times the relationship was much more personal and the overall consensus left enough space for personal expression. Berlioz suffered severely in his conservatory days, as did Debussy who, though winning a *Prix de Rome*, carried a profound dislike for all academic enterprise with him for the rest of his life. The continuous rejections Ravel received for his *Prix* entries created a public scandal resulting in the resignation of the director of the conservatory. Rimsky-Korsakov wisely did not want young Stravinsky enter the conservatory, thus recreating the old master–pupil situation, which had also served Chopin, Brahms, and Schönberg so well. Hugo Wolf was kicked out of the conservatory of Vienna, where Gustav Mahler was a close friend, and who, after some rebellion, chose to submit to its authoritarian rule, which must have been very painful for someone of his temperament. Bruckner never studied at a conservatory—which might have crushed his already low self-esteem—and only hesitatingly accepted a post as a teacher there later in his career. And it can be argued that Berg and Webern, who studied privately with Schönberg, would never have come under his spell within a conservatory context, although it has to be doubted whether that would have been, in comparison, a bad thing.

In short, unless special conditions are provided for, conditions comparable to the premodern master/student relationship, academic teaching does not seem the best environment for the development of outstanding artistic talent; it breeds conformity, mediocrity, rationality, convention, all the usual suspects for the erosion of art. In the old way of close, personal learning by imitation and direct contact with highly gifted masters, it was the passionate love and dedication toward the art form itself which was the focus, not the master's or pupil's individual originality. Both parties, master and pupil, felt subjected to the authority of the art form and its tradition of practices, so there was no need for personal rebellion. Love invites voluntary surrender. In absorbing the means of tradition, which were not an orthodox straightjacket but a carrying dynamic, the budding artist could find meaning which had already been proven by former practice and which he could make his own and give his personal interpretation. This psychological climate of mutual dedication to a common passion seems to have been the best circumstance in which the creative impulse can flourish and develop. This is light-years removed from the present cult of originality, which in most cases is either insignificant (a bad artist can be original) or indiscernible (originality only becomes visible against the backdrop of a tradition) and, ironically, fully in tune with the conformity bred at most art academies and music conservatories. Considering the requirement of originality, so often part of the curriculum, it is no surprise that these institutions turn out young artists who are every bit as original as everybody else.

The originality cult, which still is an important myth of modern art and modern music, rests upon a fundamental misunderstanding concerning what art, what art music, is and how it works. Only by recognizing the disruptive nature of the last century may it become possible to recreate or restore traditional European culture, much as the Italians did in the Renaissance with their free and dynamic revival of Antiquity. Recreation, however, is something very different from repetition, since all meaningful works of art contain both elements from their past and the contemporary fingerprints of their maker. It is therefore logical that composers of "new" tonality and "new" tradition explore the sound and means of expression of the past, but try to find a personal interpretation of them, thereby making them contemporary—contemporary in a very different way, as was fashion in the last century.

The current widespread financial crisis in the Western world, which threatens all nonprofit organizations, including art organizations (museums, orchestras, theaters, and art education), underlines the necessity to rejuvenate the tenets of new art on their most fundamental points, to begin with "meaning." In times of great change, the human mind turns inward, searching for sources of inspiration and emotional energy to be able to cope with circumstances. Given the decadence of the world of the visual arts, with its concept art absurdities and fake markets, it is to be expected that the new forms of figurative painting, which pursue real artistic and aesthetic meaning, will continue to develop and increasingly find acceptance in the wider cultural field, while all the nonsense will, under the pressures of financial realities, wither away. This is a good thing, like a winter storm blowing away the dead leaves, which would only hinder budding life in spring. In the same way, in the musical world, the funding for sonic art, an art form that is so shallow and has nothing really meaningful to contribute to culture, will disappear, maybe not entirely—but certainly its hollow pretentions to be music will be looked through quickly and thoroughly. Also, new music that is made of cheap confections from pop or world music and is not capable of communicating some sense of inward meaning cannot protect itself against the challenge of making an artistically meaningful contribution. Only new music that makes use of the means of musical communication as developed over the ages and that have formed the fundament of the central performance culture, can meet the requirements of the times. New-classical music is not merely a continuation of past practice, but a meaningful contribution to the *raison d'être* of orchestras, opera theatres, and the chamber music field: it shows the enduring need of cultural orientation and search for meaning that has always characterized cultural achievement. This need is the best justification of the musical institutions to claim funding from society, for a society with *real* culture will develop self-confidence and a positive identity, will find the capacity to make value judgments, and eventually will find workable solutions in fields different from the arts. A healthy cultural scene which cultivates meaning is a source of inspiration. As long as society accepts, tolerates, and supports nihilistic cults of self-deprecation in its midst, it will help its own downfall and will deserve its resulting misery.

SEVEN

The Cultural Shopping Mall: Pluralism and Choice

The current availability of information, in all fields, has created a unique situation for the artist. He or she can choose from a range of possibilities, wider than has ever existed before. On one hand, this is truly democratic: he or she can make a selection of techniques or principles that suits him or her best. On the other hand, the danger is that cultural forms are perceived as commodities, as *objects* which can be "possessed" and perceived as something easily obtained and manipulated, as if they were separated from their history and from their psychological, emotional, and spiritual meanings (which are not always immediately perceptible on a surface level). Therefore, the myth of the "global village" is potentially destructive as it restricts reality to a superficial present which is instantly available for consumption. It disguises the lengthy gestation process which is a condition for the development of an artistic tradition. The accessibility of the cultural object in the pluralistic culture's "shopping mall" suggests that "buying" is the same as "assimilating." What is only bought, rather than assimilated, needs no meaning, which may explain why the spiritual is absent in so much contemporary art. This emptiness is the result of the incapacity to develop a sense of interiority and value. When the idea of communicating inner experience is disposed of altogether and the ideas *behind* the work of art become more important than the work's content, the notion of art disappears and the artist easily escapes artistic value judgment. The result is then, as we can see with so-called "concept art," that only the maker's intention is left, and there is no work of art at all, only objects in front of the viewer that need extensive "explanation" because they cannot speak themselves to express something. They can only "represent" something in the same way an expensive car "represents" the wealth of its owner or a full garbage bin "represents" the lifestyle of the house in which front it stands. It is in this gap between intention and reality that the "modern artist" can step in and sell, with the help of personal image making, his or her "concepts" to ignorant buyers and cynical art speculators. The use of an ideology is most practical since it can cover up the empty space of absent artistry and help sell failure as achievement. And the same holds true for sonic art; it is the objectification of art which destroys it *as art* and which makes it suitable for the cultural shopping mall—although it finds much less innocent customers to be taken in.

So, however strongly modernism, both in the visual arts and in music, claimed to protect "high art" from contamination by vulgar commercialism, it fitted perfectly well in this consumer territory because of its materialism, and eventually it created its own form of commercialism, as can be seen in the works of Andy Warhol, Jeff Koons, or Damien Hirst. They do not "reflect" or "criticize" commercialism but wholeheartedly partake in it. This is not a degeneration from high ideals, but the total absence of any ideal whatsoever. The inevitable result of an art form that does away with aesthetics, craft, and artistic expression is this: when the entire dimension of artistic meaning is cancelled, when only the surface, the objects, are left and their verbal explanation, it thus removes itself from judgment because it cannot be judged on visual criteria. In the same way with sonic art, only the sounds are left and the "directions for use" for the listening process in the program booklet, like a manual for an unusual technological tool. Behind the developments of modernism in the arts (including music) from its early beginnings, an entire history of ideas and philosophy can be found. This trickled through the strata of the thinking elites down into the restricted brains of artists and composers longing for liberation from the past, artists who were all too happy to receive the nihilistic lessons of postmodernist philosophy, which claims that reality or meaning does not exist, but only texts which refer to each other, making the implication that reality and meaning can be "made" at will: interpretation is all there is. And if it is only interpretations that exist, this means that there are only surface phenomena and no content or substance, and that each interpretation is as good as any other. As said before, it is the Humpty Dumpty thinking of Lewis Carrol's *Through the Looking Glass*:

> "When I use a word," Humpty Dumpty said in a rather scornful tone, "it means just what I choose it to mean—neither more nor less."
> "The question is," said Alice, "whether you can make words mean so many different things."
> "The question is," said Humpty Dumpty, "which is to be master—that's all."

This makes the empty works of the untalented perfectly suited to the modern cultural shopping mall mentality of modernist nonsense.

How is it possible that so many people in the developed West show an interest in this late "fruit" of modernism: concept art, which more often than not is not only meaningless, but intentionally abject, vulgar, ridiculous, and wallowing in disgusting nonsense? This seems to be something of a mystery, because in concept art there is nothing of interest, nothing to be enjoyed. The only logical explanation is this: people who are, under the thin veneer of a superficial imitation of civilization, truly primitive and degenerate, having some money to spend as a collector, or fulfilling the position of curator of a museum for modern art, see in concept art a public approval of their inner world and thus feel relieved from any shadow of guilt about their condition. In fact, concept art offers an escape from guilt. It is a kind of fake "religion" where one can get absolution without having to change anything or to make any effort. That this public approval of such barbarism is, in itself, a danger to society, will be clear: it communicates the message of nihilism, cynicism, and degeneration of the human being, as something to be admired, bought, exhibited, and with which to get rich. Concept art is happily and cynically heralding the fall of civilization itself, as in the late period of the Roman Empire when public officials were openly recommending their citizens to drop any pretence of civilization and just follow their animal appetites. The immense irony is, of course, that modernism had begun as a strong stand against degeneration. It ended, however, in the stench of a decadent swamp, where commercialism served as the instrument to spread the mud. Concept art operates in a small, ridiculous world where meaning has evaporated, where the world has become empty, and thus—from a psychological point of view—unreal, too unreal for the human being to flourish.

Real cultural traditions, however, which carry with them ages of experience, operate in a totally different territory. They refer to real reality, to the real world as perceived by the entire human being and not only by his animalistic side, and they refer to real inner experience—which leads to this conclusion: that the best artists can do in the current situation is choosing a real cultural tradition and working themselves through its world, which provides them with the tools to make value judgments beyond the surface of appearances. While on one hand the availability of so many cultural traditions is a great advantage, it can only be of fruitful use if the artist fully embraces a tradition and makes it fully *his own*, so that he becomes part of this tradition, identifies with it, thus making it authentic and contemporary and thus carrying the tradition further by injecting it with his own life experience.

The current situation can be called "postmodern" not in the sense of a style, which it cannot be, but in the sense of living in a time after a period which was dominated by modernism, the *grand récit* of the last century. We know too much to be able to construct a unified paradigm in which all information finds a happy place, there is too much difference, too many conflicting and mutually exclusive traditions, and too many different value systems. We cannot forget what we already know, as Boulez would have it, and undo this ocean of knowledge. It is a source of great richness for the artist, although also problematic because this means that the basis of his or her artistic language is no longer a neutral point of departure. He or she has to make *a priori* value judgments as to the material he or she is going to use. This creates the problem of artistic freedom: which material would be appropriate and for which reason? In the current pluralistic situation, composers can choose from whatever source the material they would like to use, with the result that the available range of possibilities is something like a holistic continuum where past and present, nearby and faraway mingle. However attractive this at first sight may be, it is only a first stage in the process of developing a way of creating meaningful music. Within this continuum, specific choices have to be made to create a personal and useful "language." In former, pre-1900 times, composers could choose basic materials from a common practice and create their personal interpretation of them, thus adding to the field of possibilities. When all traces of a living tradition have vanished, the total freedom of the situation forces the contemporary composer to freely choose his own restrictions and concentrate upon the things closest to his temperament and taste. Only in self-chosen restriction and in modeling his language upon the best possible achievements of what is already there can he hope to avoid the superficial shopping mall mentality and to develop a meaningful and personal music. The trendy mixing of things from every direction, without distinction in terms of quality, taste, culture, will tend to lead to a situation where the different elements neutralize each other, like a soup with too many ingredients or a painting with *all* available colors in it (which leads to a muddy brown with unpleasant associations). The *embarras de choix* is the typical problem of today, which, however, is by all means preferable to the totalitarian nonsense of last century's modernism.

Following this psychological and artistic logic, the contemporary classical composer has decided to create his own inner aesthetic context, based upon the tools of a tradition that suits him or her best. This means focusing upon the world of inner experience and excluding things which do not harmonize with it. In the modern world, this is no easy thing, precisely because of the presence of so many different worlds of experience, a luxury former ages did not have. Artists who pursue artistic and expressive meaning in their work can only find the means for their development within a tradition and this is why artists, who, like everybody else are the children of the modern world, in spite of all those availabilities yet seem to "turn away" from the shopping mall and pick up a tradition that may seem a restriction to the outer world. But this is only the surface—in reality they find liberation and great riches.

Cultures are no longer restricted to a certain locality or a closed tradition (i.e., a tradition with no links to the outer world). In the current pluralistic and globalized situation, many different cultural communities may live in one single town, and in Europe, many of them may have become Europeanized while keeping their cultural roots intact. After European culture intruded into the east and the south, many people from formerly colonized areas sought a future in the Western world. Sometimes one sees these different cultures living side by side. Sometimes they seem to blend. Sometimes there is opposition and conflict. In all cases, the *boundaries* between these cultures have become transparent; the "other culture" has become "visible." This does not mean that the identity of each of these cultures has diminished, for cultural identity is autonomous, in the same way that a person has a distinctive and undeniable character. Although relations between cultures can erode each group's sense of identity, this is not an inevitable process—and neither is it something positive or negative *a priori*. The character of a traditional culture may have vague boundaries but this does not mean it has no definite nature. Just as a person with a specific character may evolve dramatically through life experiences and still keep his identity (or obtain a stronger identity), so cultures may develop in various ways without losing touch with their fundamentals, which are in themselves flexible and can be adapted to circumstance. This is an important consideration, because the continuity of these fundamentals creates a core of stability and a body of values and norms, which make personal growth and development possible. The industrial age has done great damage by uprooting the identity of so many cultures and giving back things that often were valuable, but not on the level of culture and identity; material and technical progress operate on quite another level than the psychology of the individual human being.

By now, it may be clear why the distinction between a cultural tradition and modernity is so important. Most of the elements of daily life that define "the modern world," the lifestyle, technologies, and the way "modern society" organizes itself as developed in the West, operate on the material level, where logistics and technical means are supposed to make life easier. But the car, the vacuum cleaner, the computer, the microwave, and the credit card do not touch the inner world of the individual. This may seem a trivial observation, but many people derive from the manifold appearances of modernity a sense of culture, of being part of a network of values that is suggested by the blinking and smooth surface of "the modern world," intensified by the images of commerce and advertisement, which celebrate immature consumer fantasies. Even modern gadgets, which fulfill a reasonable function, are often clothed in the aesthetics that evoke the utopian dreams of a world in which everything is possible and all hindrances are removed.

Even at its best, modernity is not culture but surface functionalism. It is on the level of inner experience that a cultural tradition operates and this can be a world apart from "modernity," which has no roots, and thus can easily be introduced everywhere in the world (with the result that all "modern cities" in the world look more or less the same and, in general terms, operate in the same way). It is the technical and material surface level of life, not the inner life of the human being. Everywhere where the modern world dominates, cultural traditions erode because many people are drawn to the surface of things, impressed by modern technology. And this is not only the fate of Eastern or African cultures; it is also European culture that suffers from modernity, although Europe was the cradle of the modern world with the first industrial revolution in England. Right from the beginning, it was clear that, apart from the obvious material advantages, it was also damaging a fragile way of life—a life with bad as well as good things. Right from the start, artists, poets, and writers have warned against the side effects of modernity because they felt a conflict here between two levels of experience: on one hand, practical and material progress—which were often benign—and an erosion of the spiritual and aspirational side of life on the other. This rubbing of two different worlds created, in the nineteenth century, the great upsurge of poetry, art, and especially music (the art of interiority *par excellence*), often in protest against these negative side effects of modernity (while sometimes borrowing from its utopian rhetoric). If we can see that the conflict between cultural traditions and modernity, which creates so much tension in the non-Western world, is the same conflict which played such an important role in Western history of the twentieth century, then we can look into European/Western cultural traditions with a more objective eye. It may then become clearer which cultural expressions are, for Westerners, more meaningful than others, and a hierarchy of values will then gradually appear with which distinctions and judgments can be made in the superficial shopping mall of pluralism. Then, the surface becomes transparent and the important things behind the "maya" of the "market place" may become visible.

The negative effects of modernity upon the inner life of the human being have profound consequences. The erosion of cultural identity and the human scale of life destroys the focus and perspective that was accumulated during the experience of past generations. Their experiences may seem to lose their meaning in new circumstances where a surface reality that is disconnected from the inner life seems so strongly present. Much more than in former periods, with modernity there has grown a conflict between inner and outer reality. If cultural and social environments are insecure, within a context of surface modernity there is no place where new, durable insights can be developed, insights which can be interpreted in different individual situations, but which are based upon comparable experiences in the past. In such a situation, a strong cultural identity can offer, among other things, a point of reference, a center of stability and permanence through which life can again become meaningful and worthwhile, providing a background of values for understanding, development, and action. (We see this process with immigrants who sport their original culture more ostentatiously in a foreign country than in their country of origin.) It is here that the role of the artist within society takes on a new form. Instead of an isolated individual, living and working exclusively according to his or her own private norms and values, he or she can create the symbols through which a wider group of people can find their identity. It is the artist's capacity to define his or her identity within the referential framework of some kind of common culture which makes art socially relevant and important, because such an artist can share his or her experiences in a profound way with individuals, who can measure their own experiences against those expressions and thus, literally, find out who and what they really are. In this way, art—real art—can provide an inner space where the process of civilization and cultivation can take place, according to every individual's capacities and needs. So, in the multicultural context of today, in which the artist can no longer simply embrace his or her inherited culture unquestioningly, his or her function as a creator of symbols of coherence, meaning, and identity, therefore becomes increasingly essential to the spiritual life of communities and their individual members. It means that new classical music, like new figurative painting and new classical architecture, can again create a socially and psychologically relevant art, an art which reveals and confirms European cultural identity and civilizational values, an art with deep roots into the past, an art which is capable of infinite development and variation, an art with a timeless quality and thus contemporary forever.

Like modernism in art, the project of modernity in general has begun to disintegrate toward the end of the twentieth century under the weight of its own contradictions. Knowledge of the wider world has resulted in an awareness of the limits and relativity of Western thought. In the past, the passion for inquiry and riches led European culture to impose itself in places where it had nothing to seek. Disaster after disaster has revealed its weaknesses and forced the West to concede the possible validity of other points of view. The confrontation with the variegation of the world has generated doubts as to whether European culture as a whole has any claims to universality, since we have come to understand that each culture has its own intrinsic value and should be respected as such. But this respect does not imply that there are no universal civilization values; it is in those values that also can be recognized in other cultures that elements of European culture can be considered universal. These values will be at the heart of every important civilization and paradoxically, *neutral*. They refer to what is timeless in the human being and to what is possible in any culture when it aspires to develop to the heights of the spirit. This universalism is fundamentally different from the "universalism" of modernity, which operates at the surface of life. It is also different from the idea of "cultural relativism" (as we have seen in chapter 6), which denies the possibility of value judgment in terms of levels of civilization. There obviously exist different levels of development everywhere, but they cannot simply be attributed to cultures as a whole—they can be found in every culture according to the kind of society in which they find themselves. As history shows, the level of civilized values goes up and down, under the pressures of circumstances, mentality of people, climatological factors, and the like.

During the heyday of modernism in the arts in the 1950s and 1960s, already the first signs of protest against any quasi-scientific certainty began to show. Pop art, happenings, and populist critique of modernism's steel-like idealism could be seen as the first expressions of what later was described as "postmodernism." There are many definitions of postmodernism, and they are often themselves postmodern in their shallowness, vagueness, and fragmented eclecticism. On one level, postmodernism refers to the awareness that modernism was a more or less closed period with more or less closed ideologies—so, the description of a situation after a period of modernism, not of an aesthetic or artistic trend. But used as an artistic "idea," it means merely the giving up of any high ideal, of the demarcation lines between present and past, between different styles, different cultures, and especially between "high" and "low" culture. It is the vision of the cultural shopping mall, where only the surface of things—the commercial appearances—count. It is a primitive mindset unworthy of serious consideration, with roots in dada, surrealism, and the teenage cult. But it is noteworthy that this mindset perfectly harmonized with cultural relativity: anything goes, whatever reaches the mind is at best entertainment, and nothing more—"there is no value and no meaning."

The many cultures of the present and the past which are accessible to us often seem mutually exclusive. This contrasts with pre-industrial times, when a cultural consensus in European society was generally intact, because the minor influences from non-European territories did not undermine general agreements of cultural values and were absorbed and "Europeanized." In the present, such greater awareness of other cultures forces us to think about our own culture in ways which are new, because the context is new. Sometimes the question is asked, under the influence of cultural relativism, whether European traditional culture should be dominant in modern Europe. Although it would be absurd to question the centrality of European culture in Europe itself, as it would be as absurd to ask the same kind of question in relation to, for instance, India or China ("should Indian culture be dominant in India?"), it is clear that the presence of other cultures around the center of European culture in Europe itself is an enrichment, as long as it does not undermine a general cultural consensus of what is European. And it is to be expected that non-European cultures within Europe will, in the course of time, to some extent Europeanize, although it is at this stage difficult to determine what this means in practice. Time will tell—and it is to be hoped that Europe will not break down as a result of its own cultural insecurity in combination with the weight of foreign influences, gradually eroding European cultural identity and its civilization, as happened in the later periods of the Roman Empire (before the mass migrations) when a similar kind of multiculturalism and internationalism changed the nature of Hellenistic Antiquity.

At this point, the question of how a new form of classical music could be compatible with the modern world, has to be addressed. How could a musical tradition, embodying values of a bygone world, be meaningful in the twenty-first century? The assertion that art, and in this case, art music, should reflect the present times, the times in which the listeners live themselves, suggests a direct relationship that is not only nonsensical (contemporary art is already from the present by fact) but also dangerous. Given the overall erosion of civilization in the modern Western world, reflecting contemporaneity is obviously not a good thing. It is one of the eroding results of historicist thinking which maintains as an axiom that history develops in linear fashion, and ever progressively and automatically, toward a better future. But history itself shows plainly that a highly developed civilization can easily decline into barbarism, losing the achievements of numerous generations. This did not only happen in the last century. As Bryan Ward-Perkins writes in *The Fall of Rome and the End of Civilization*:

> The end of the Roman West witnessed horrors and dislocation of a kind I sincerely hope never to have to live through; and it destroyed a complex civilization, throwing the inhabitants of the West back to a standard of living typical of prehistoric times. Romans before the fall were as certain as we are today that their world would continue for ever substantially unchanged. They were wrong. We would be wise not to repeat their complacency. (p. 183)

Traditional values, in any context and in any field, are by themselves not meaningful just for the reason that they are traditional. As the French poet René Char has said, "Our inheritance has come to us without a testament." The challenge for the artist is to find values in the vast storehouse of the past which can be applied again in the present and this depends upon two factors: (1) whether they are universals, that is, meaningful independent of time and place, and (2) whether specific values are particularly meaningful at this moment in the present. And, of course, both factors may be in play. In music, the intention of writing meaningful music is in itself not a problem—but problems arise when language is considered. Some things are only expressible if a musical language exists that can function as an effective vehicle for meaning; in this sense, music is like language. But if certain universal, human experiences can only be expressed in a musical language that seems to belong to the past, when it was normal to express these things, the necessity arises to take this musical language as a starting point.

Thus, the question arises about *style*: could a contemporary composer write music in a style that was developed in the past and still seriously *mean* what is expressed (i.e., could he or she still be authentic?)? This question is related to another: is there no contradiction in driving to a concert in a car and then listening to Bach on replicas of eighteenth-century instruments in an air-conditioned atmosphere under sophisticated electric lighting? Or listening to a Beethoven symphony played on a CD set? Is *playing* a "new classical work" comparable with playing a genuine "old" work, and aren't both something like parading oneself with a wig or dressed up as a visitor to a Parisian salon in the nineteenth century? The answers to these questions are obvious. . . . Performing a work from the "old" repertoire is fundamentally no different from *composing* in an older style, or interpreting an older style. "Old" works function in the present because they are based upon universal human experience; the identity of a musical work is not found in the means—the sound material, but in the end—the expressive "message," which is a musical one. A work's identity is its living and expressive character, and this can be called its "soul," its "personality." Its nature is spiritual, like the nature of the human being. Neither the score, nor the performance "is" the work in this sense: they are the presentations of the work, which is itself independent of place and time. Also its style is not totally locked up in the context from which it had developed, hence our capacity to understand its musical language. So, there is no real difference between a composer who—at the beginning of the twenty-first century—writes in a style reminiscent of Prokofiev or Bartok, and a composer in the twentieth century who uses a rather "old-fashioned" musical language, like Britten or Shostakovich. One is reminded of Brahms, who stubbornly stuck to a style, in the late nineteenth century, that had been developed at the beginning of that century. Yet, he developed it in his own, personal way, reinterpreted it, and thus made it authentic and for its time contemporary. Also his music happened to give a hint to Schönberg, who quasi-catapulted Brahms into modernity in his famous essay, "Brahms the Progressive" (1947). Surely Brahms himself would have been quite surprised to find out about this result of his influence.

An example that underlines the relativity of cultural styles in the context of their period is the so-called Augustan Renaissance in the period of the rule of the first Roman emperor, Augustus. The 500-year-old Roman Republic (510 BC–1st century BC), which preceded it, had been weakened by the civil wars of the Late Republic after the murder of Julius Caesar. When Augustus finally won power, his main efforts were invested in creating peace and stability, resulting in the long period that would be known as Pax Romana, which was later celebrated as the dawn of a Golden Age by Virgil in the *Aeneid*. This period was an era of relative tranquillity in which Rome endured neither major civil wars, such as the perpetual bloodshed of the third century AD, nor serious invasions, such as those of the Second Punic War three centuries prior. The arts, after a rather demoralized, meagre time, flourished anew, and interestingly, they were classicist in nature: sculptors and architects took up earlier Hellenistic examples and interpreted them anew, as can be seen in the marvellous *Ara Pacis*, the Altar for Peace, erected in 9 BC. After such a long time of disruption and insecurity, people longed for stability and peace and naturally this found expression in an art which emanated and symbolized this harmony. This happened after already *ages* of Hellenistic art (i.e., after a long period of renewed interpretations of the same artistic tradition). Was this Pax Romana a "conservative," restrictive cultural period? By no means—it went down as one of the most artistically successful periods of Roman civilization. Elements from Greek culture were taken as examples not *because* they were old, or *in spite of* their antiquity, but simply because these elements best expressed what needed to be expressed at the time. The motivation was not something historical but something universal: what worked well for the Greeks would work well for the Romans after a period of serious erosion of their society. The Hellenistic nature of this art became a symbol of renewal and the restoration of civilizational values. In this example, the concept of a living, freely interpreted tradition worked wonderfully well. In the context of the time, it seems very unlikely that anybody would have complained that the style of the new art was so old fashioned—much more important considerations took precedence.

It can be argued that the present composers of new classical music are similarly much more concerned, consciously or subconsciously, about restoring something precious from a highly developed civilization than about "being modern" or "up-to-date," which indeed seems meaningless in the present cultural situation. And in rejecting the clichés from the last century, they unintentionally *become* up-to-date, because their work is directly related to the present cultural questions.

When we talk about style in art music, it is helpful to look to other art forms, because in terms of style all art is the result of structuring, of *design*. As the short exploration in art history above shows, the use of elements from the past is nothing special, and if we dig deeper in the history of cultural traditions, it appears to be a regular feature rather than an exception. In Renaissance and later periods of painting, historic scenes were often furnished with elements from older periods; backgrounds in portraiture often depicted imaginary buildings from antiquity. And in architecture, there has been a constant reinterpretation of older forms and structures, sometimes from mutually exclusive stylistic fields, like the

Pantheon in Paris, of which the exterior strives after an imagined "Greek" character—that is, plain, almost without ornaments, grand but simple, while in the interior the architect has intentionally tried to combine the lightness and grace of medieval gothic churches with the rich visual language of late eighteenth-century ornamentation, both in extreme contrast to the exterior; yet, the whole makes a beautiful and harmonious effect. Another, rather extreme but fully convincing example is the Karlskirche in Vienna, which combines two free-standing pillars and a strict temple front inspired by Roman times with a contemporary Baroque structure and ornamentation in the rest of the building. Eastern cultures like India or the Arabian world use traditional forms in their new buildings and life style without problems, and where people are endowed with taste, the "modern" is not intrusive and mostly hidden behind a traditional surface that shows the continuity of an environment in which descendents of a rich culture feel comfortable, without having to suffer from the technical shortcomings of the past. The modernist idea that modern life should be an overall demonstration of functionalist "ideals," with chrome, steel, glass, and square forms everywhere, was hopelessly naive and sentimental and in gross contradiction to the realities of life and the universals of cultural traditions. Especially the rejection of ornamentation in favor of "functionalism" proves modernism's materialist approach, as if ornaments would not fulfill a function—only, it would be not a materialist function but a psychological and aesthetic one. So, the question whether a new classical music has a legitimate place in contemporary life is a non-question, since the classical revolution advocates a return to normality and offers an invitation to step out of the closed box of prejudice as created by the last century. Within the pluralist reality of modern life, the classical tradition—both in its canonic repertoire and its new forms— offers a richness of inner experience that compensates for its absence in the surface reality of the contemporary world. It meets a profound need and is therefore today the most contemporary form of art music—including its canonic "museum" repertoire.

It is an encouraging sign that in painting, all kinds of new realism are increasingly being accepted by museums, treated more seriously by art historians, and are no longer the exclusive "property" of commercial art galleries. The Florence Academy of Art, the Grand Central Academy of Art in New York, and the London Atelier of Representational Art are some of the educational institutions that emerge at many places to answer an increasing demand for education in traditional craft. And yes, this kind of education is institutionalized since the master–pupil relationship seems, alas, to be economically not viable nowadays. As said before, in architecture there also have been attempts to revive traditional building, of which the two early pioneers, Leon Krier and Quinlan Terry, stand out as the most remarkable; sounds like Le Corbusier's plans to demolish the old center of Paris and replace it with futuristic tower blocks are no longer heard. In the English-speaking world, the successful company, Adam Architecture, led by the classically minded architect Robert Adam, shows convincingly how one can build in a classical style in the present time (www.adamarchitecture.com).

But where are the music festivals offering a platform for new classical music with concerts, debates, explorations, workshops? Where is the public space that can be enlightened by the torch bearers of a new musical century?

EIGHT

Conclusion: The Debate about Beauty

The emergence of new forms of the classical tradition in Europe (in the visual arts, in architecture, and in music) have consequences for the way in which culture in this tortured continent is considered. Also, it forces us to reconsider some of the unpondered orthodoxies of the musical establishment, not in the least because, over the last years, a debate has emerged in philosophy and aesthetics about the concept of beauty in relation to the contemporary world, with important contributions by some brilliant authors:

- Alexander Nehamas: *Only a Promise of Happiness: The Place of Beauty in a World of Art*
- Roger Scruton: *Beauty*
- Paolo Euron: *Art, Beauty and Imitation: An Outline of Aesthetics*
- Denis Dutton: *The Art Instinct: Beauty, Pleasure & Human Evolution*
- Andreas Dorschel (ed.): *Gemurmel unterhalb des Rauschens: Theodor W. Adorno und Richard Strauss*

(Further details can be found in the Further Reading section at the end.)

Beauty is back on the agenda of a broader cultural discussion and so is beauty in music, because within the context of the classical tradition, beauty is a normal, if not always the most important ingredient. Contrary to what has become a conventional idea in the last century, beauty is *not* necessarily always kitsch or cheap commercialism. The most difficult form of beauty is one which is a result of authenticity. Given the fact that there are so many ways in which beauty is presented and so many different interpretations of the notion, it is a rewarding field of both philosophical enquiry and artistic creation. In the modern world where real, authentic beauty is such a rare phenomenon, composers find it worthwhile to pursue it, even if it sometimes may remain a promising vision at some eternal day break—in the process of trying to reach it, beauty is created along the way.

It has been said (by, among others, Roger Scruton in his *Aesthetics of Music*) that in the modern world, the psychological and emotional innocence and purity which are preconditions of real, authentic beauty—as can be experienced in Bach, Mozart, Debussy, and in some works of Mahler—has disappeared. But could this be true? Is it not a universal capacity of the human being independent of circumstances? This superior form of beauty should not be confused with naivety. On the contrary, it is an ultimate *knowing* of something. It is the result of being in touch with a spiritual realm which always eludes complete realization on this earth, but serves as a source of inspiration for beauty and artistic meaning. All the more spectacular that it is here at all, in the great works of great artists, in spite of everything that seems to deny it and to besmear it as an intrusive element that has to be destroyed. The beauty we recognize in this so often seemingly meaningless world, is not of this world; it is the fingerprint of a sacred presence, a creative force "behind" reality, to remind us of where we came from and to where we, eventually, will go. It is the task of the artist to illuminate, to beautify and ennoble our life experiences, including its pain, so that our inner life stays alive during "the journey from coast to coast," as the Indian mystic Rabindranath Tagore described the human condition. Beauty keeps the inner connection with our destiny intact.

Debussy once said, "To some people, the mere attempt to create beauty is taken as a personal insult." In an ugly age, real and authentic beauty is indeed an insult, it insults the generally accepted ugliness: by its inner light, it exposes the real nature of the surrounding ugliness to the full—and this may be unbearable for people who try to get used to it in order to be able to get on in the world. Inevitably, the really gifted composers of new classical music challenge received wisdom that accepts and installs ugliness as the legitimate "expression" of the modern world. Adorno was very wrong when he condemned, in his *Philosophy of New Music* (1949), Stravinsky for his "providing entertainment for the bourgeoisie," and presented Schönberg with all his "true and honest" ugliness as the only way in which the ugly modern world could find authentic, ugly expression in art music. According to Adorno, after the Holocaust, beauty in music and poetry could only be a lie, a statement echoed many times and eventually petrified into a cliché; what could be excused as a genuine moral and emotional reaction after the catastrophe of World War II became a convention for later generations of artists who did not have any experience of the war but discovered in this moralizing prescription the attractive opportunity to flaunt their own inability to create beauty as an asset, thus creating the sinister spectacle of "artists" (including composers) taking a moralist stand against the wrongs of the world by amply contributing to its ugliness. In such a climate, a psychological healing of a conventionalized, institutionalized war trauma is not an easy thing to do, as attempts in that direction were—and still often are—stopped in their tracks as immoral acts by the establishment: the world upside down and inside out, a veritable inversion of meaning and value.

The shadow of the Holocaust should not prevent beauty from emerging again, after a period of mourning, to contribute to the healing of European/Western civilization. It is an absurd idea that an ugly truth would protect the traditions of high culture from contamination with the trivialities of modern life. Adorno was not only wrong in a general sense but also wrong in relation to the twentieth century. As Ravel innocently asked in the 1930s, when people around him asserted that the first thing a composer should want to do was to express his own time: "Why should an ugly time need expression?'

In this time of redefinition for Europe, of its cultural identity and the political future of its society, it is about time that the cultural achievements of the past and their progeny in the present are given their rightful place and role in public space (which would also have implications for American music life). Performing bodies of classical art music should not—under the pressure of economic crises—be subjected to materialist profit assessment and thus to government cuts, but instead be generously supported as iconic spaces which would justify any financial sacrifice. The humanities at the universities, where cultural studies are taught, should likewise be considered as important for society as a whole and not subjected to economic functionalism or pragmatism; understanding of the best of art (particularly from the past) should be a normal part of the curriculum at every level of general education, including for young children. Also—and particularly—in times of economic hardship, art (i.e., *real and meaningful* art), should be the island of civilization where people will drink at the well of real humanity so that they can be able to face the challenges of modern life and protect the values of the human spirit. High art is an exercise of what is best in the human being. It offers a learning process of the intellect and the emotions that can lead to an increased awareness of what we really are and should be, and, as such, a source of inner strength. It was exactly *this* role that the classical music repertoire played in World War II and in the period directly following this fundamental crisis; it would be unthinkable that people would scramble among the ruins of bombed city centers, desperate to hear a performance of Xenakis, Stockhausen, or Boulez (or in a later period along the glass and steel façades of modernist office blocks to hear the sonic art of Lachenmann, Widmann, or Birtwistle) hoping to be uplifted and to feel again what it means to be a human being. Their work is a product of, not an answer to, the devastation of war trauma and the emptiness of the modern world. If we allow sonic art to be music, we finish off the jobs of destruction set in motion by Hitler and Stalin. Britten's *War Requiem* was the right answer to that destruction, also in terms of beauty—and the most important works of far-reaching implications just after the war were, from our perspective of the early twenty-first century, not the sound art of Boulez's *Marteau sans maitre* (1954), or Stockhausen's *Gesang der Jünglinge* (1956), or Nono's *Il canto sospeso* (1956), but Britten's *Peter Grimes* (1945) and Shostakovich's *1st Violin Concerto* (1948), both works now in the regular repertoire and still growing in stature and reputation. And perhaps the piece that has been, with hindsight and in psychological terms, the most far reaching in its stubborn faith in humanity, beauty, and the immortality of the soul, is that unexpected flowering of pure and beautiful expression, hovering over the ruins of a destroyed civilization, the last gasp of atonement of a man who saw his world go down but yet believed in the endurance of its best achievements in another, better world: Richard Strauss' *Vier Letzte Lieder* (1948).

NINE

Some Composers

Here, at the end of this journey through rather virginal territory, it is appropriate to introduce some composers of new classical music. The list is not comprehensive or representative and must be seen as merely a handful of interesting examples which are worthy of further exploration. Composers who have already made some explorations into a more traditional, tonal idiom, like Americans John Corigliano, David del Tredici, and the later John Adams, are not considered here because there is already enough information about them available elsewhere and their music is not classical in the sense set forth in the previous chapters. Like the English composer Robin Holloway, they often have a strong attachment to typical twentieth-century ways of engineering the musical surface and are not much interested in the aesthetic and philosophical possibilities of the concept of "classicism." The same can be said of composers like Magnus Lindberg, who made a name in the sonic field but eventually developed into something like an almost musical Boulez, as can be heard in his *Fresco* and *Cantigas*. Yet, without these composers it would, maybe, have been more difficult for a more classically orientated music to emerge. Of all the mentioned composers it must be underlined that, although influences of premodernist traditions can clearly be heard, they have been able to forge a musical language which is all their own. When, in the following descriptions, other well-known composers are mentioned, this does not refer to a literal likeness but indicates an association as to the psychological and stylistic world which is close to the composers' heart and will thus give some impression to the reader.

Since artists do not live in a void, influences are normal, but far more important is the individual interpretation and synthesizing of these influences. This combination of personal elements and material from a tradition: the personal handling of a tradition or multiple traditions, is not a defect in invention or imagination, but the opposite. In existing material, possibilities of further development are heard and this is exactly how an artistic tradition works. Their originality shows in every detail of their music, stamping the material with their own character. This process is very different from the conventional "new music," which is so often characterized, in spite of colorful surfaces, by an impersonal blandness, the result of so many people trying to be as original as everybody else on a material level, instead of trying to find a personal expression on a psychological level. This lack of interiority and personal character cannot be compensated for by whatever complexity or eccentricity on the sound surface, an observation which incidentally also counts for new classical music.

Of course, as is the case with every kind of music, there is new classical music around that has only mediocre qualities. Still, it is less painful and embarrassing to have to listen to mediocre new classical music than, dependent upon the level of pain one is able to endure, to mediocre sonic art. And also new classical music has its "white noise" in the form of dilettanti who thoughtlessly rumble around in the triadic collections of the repertoire. The presence of the classical tradition in the background, however, means that such people can be heard through quickly when measured up to real craft and personality, a filter absent in sonic art. The following composers are all operating on a level above these deficiencies, and their qualities are increasingly recognized in concert life, which is a hopeful sign that it will be possible to restore the credibility of contemporary music to audiences and performers alike. Some composers have audio samples on their sites, others only information; when no site is indicated, further information can be found elsewhere via internet search programs or at the relevant national music information centers.

Also it has to be said that possibly not all mentioned composers would fully and completely endorse everything said in this book. They do not carry any responsibility for the text, other than having inspired it by their music, as it appeared in public space. An artist does not first develop a philosophy and then set out to demonstrate it in works of art. Often artists are not fully aware of what they are doing or of the implications of what they are doing. In isolated cases when artists first theorize and then practice, as with Richard Wagner, artistic reality does not always fit the theories. The writer of these lines could only describe the philosophy of new classical music after a life of experience in the art form, during which gradually the whole picture of what was happening was emerging. All the composers mentioned hereafter may have different ways of describing their work, as far as they write about it at all, like Nicolas Bacri, who happens to also be a gifted writer about music. The most natural reaction of an artist, questioned about the philosophical background of his art, is this: why should I have to explain it if I have already created it? A work of art has more meaning than can be said in words, which does not make interpretation superfluous but offers multiple paths to discover the meaning and the implications of the creative act in the world around it.

NICOLAS BACRI

The Frenchman Nicolas Bacri (www.nicolasbacri.net) has a penchant for concerti, of which should certainly be mentioned his brilliant and expressive *Concerto for Flute and Orchestra* and *Third Violin Concerto*. His music combines a strongly lyrical expressivity with a harmonic idiom that travels from dissonant combinations to triadic tonalities. The compactness of his language and the motivic developments of his material evokes German influences, like early Schönberg, as his motoric passages link it to music like Shostakovich's, but his feeling for refined coloring underline his alliance with the French tonal traditions. Obviously, Bacri is the most important French composer since Messiaen and Dutilleux, leaving the sonics far behind.

JAMES FRANCIS BROWN

J. F. Brown (www.jamesfrancisbrown.com) is a young British composer who, like David Matthews, felt stimulated by the music of Benjamin Britten and Michael Tippett, but who also absorbed international influences like Bartok and Busoni, and welded these into a musical language with a strongly composed structure and broad narratives, through which the dynamic possibilities of tonal expression and coloring are exploited to the full. Sometimes his music has an Eastern-European rhythmic "bite," as in his monumental and impressive *Piano Quartet*, which has been included in his recent chamber music CD "Prospero's Isle" (Guild, 2011).

RICHARD DUBUGNON

Richard Dubugnon (www.richarddubugnon.com) is a French/Swiss composer living in Paris. His music is characterized by a virtuoso, colorful surface, sometimes close to Dutilleux but with more fluency and suppleness, which shows the benign influence of the music of Debussy and Scriabine. The "bite" of some works relates them to Russian composers like Prokoviev and Shostakovich, as does the harmonic vocabulary. His extensive cycle of orchestral pieces based upon the tarot cards, *Arcanes Symphoniques*, shows a composer with an unbridled phantasy for textures and moods.

DAVID MATTHEWS

The Englishman David Matthews (www.david-matthews.co.uk), brother of modernist composer Colin Matthews, could be considered a follower of Benjamin Britten, who together with Shostakovich kept up what was left of the European tradition in a time when this was considered anathema. Matthews' delicate orchestral textures and (sometimes classical) forms show poetic but also well-structured narratives, of which the romanticism is sometimes close to music like Sibelius' or Mahler's. His oeuvre consists of symphonies, concerti, symphonic poems, and chamber music that show the viability of English traditions and their adaptability to new interpretation.

ALAN MILLS

Alan Mills is one of those artists who show the strong connection between the cultural traditions of Ireland, where he was born, and France (like many Irish artists), which inspired him to seek his roots in the climate of the 1920s, when the Parisian scene flourished in a wide range of musical styles, of which the "Group des Six" was the most striking. Mills' music sometimes sounds close to Poulenc's, but is more complex and rhythmically dense, developing aspects which had been neglected by "Les Six." His songs on French texts are particularly striking and effective. Mills is based in London.

JEFF HAMBURG

The American composer Jeff Hamburg (www.jeffhamburg.com) settled in the Netherlands, where he found and explored his Jewish roots, resulting in a lyrical idiom where folkloristic elements mix with traditional forms, realized in a colorful orchestral treatment which gives ample space to an expressive and intense lyricism. The music is often built in layers, covering wide panels of sound that sometimes evoke Sibelius or Ravel. The exoticism makes use of modal colorings, decorative arabesques, but always in the service of expression. He writes orchestral works (with or without voice), music theatre, and chamber music.

WOLFGANG-ANDREAS SCHULTZ

Although Schultz (former student of Ligeti) is not a typical "classical composer" as described in this book, he should be mentioned here because his work signifies a profound change in compositional thinking in contemporary Germany, the country having suffered most from the plight of modernism as a "moral proof" that the dark recent past has been overcome. Apart from being a brilliant and profound theorist, Schultz has experimented with the idea of returning to traditional compositional practice from an overall vision of total integration of different cultural frameworks in terms of historical periods and geography. In this holistic music, elements from Western tonal traditions, modernist atonalism, and Eastern traditions, are synthesized according to a complex technique that is determined by a psychological and spiritual vision. Much of his utopian project includes a return toward traditional musical thinking, based upon his understanding of classical music, but it is part of an idea the boundaries of which extend further than can be defined by the European classical tradition. (www.wolfgangandreasschultz.de)

WOLFRAM WAGNER

Wolfram Wagner (www.wolfram-wagner.com; no relations to the nineteenth-century composer) is a Viennese composer who has his musical roots in the 1920s and medieval music. He commands an expressive range from colorful fantasy (the ballet music *Phantastische Szenen*) to ritualistic severity (*Augustinus Oratorium*), in an original idiom where influences of the later Schreker, Hindemith, and Pärt find unexpected and expressive confluence.

REZA VALI

The American composer Reza Vali (www.rezavali.com), who was born in Iran and studied in Vienna, eventually settled in Pittsburgh, where he teaches at Carnegie Mellon University. Using Iranian folk material, he welded an expressive and lyrical language using European tonal traditions to create narrative and motivic unfolding, a synthesis which (in terms of intention) could be compared to Bartok's, who, in a similar way, subjected material he found during his long research journeys through the Balkans to a treatment derived from the classical tradition. Vali's impressive orchestral song cycle *The Being of Love,* based on Iranian poetry, shows a composer who has fully absorbed Western ways of handling all the parameters of tonality without losing the exotic atmosphere and intense emotionalism of his Persian heritage.

HANS KOX

However provincial the Netherlands are, and however strongly modernism and all its pitfalls have dominated its musical production in the second half of the twentieth century, one composer stands out with an original oeuvre which combines an independent, traditionally orientated creative mind with a lively receptivity toward contemporary materials: Hans Kox (www.hanskox.nl).

Only parts of his oeuvre can be called "new classical music," of which should be mentioned his impressive *Anne Frank Cantata* and the oratorio *Shoa*, with very expressive choruses in the tradition of Bach's passions and cantatas, and his *Third Violin Concerto*, in which he similarly fuses traditional, almost-baroque elements with an almost-expressionistic tonality. In general, Kox's effective music is experimental in character, also in the direction of the classical tradition. His achievement is that, in an environment in which this was anathema, he always used whatever elements were available as means of expression.

JOHN BORSTLAP

And last but not least, John Borstlap (www.johnborstlap.com), who strives after an expressive and pure classicism in a development which started out with Schönbergian influences and which gradually explored more and more classical idioms and forms. Rooted in the German tonal traditions, his music has always been open to French (and sometimes Eastern) influences, coloring harmony, and instrumental treatment. His works show that it is possible to write an authentic music while using elements from the past, turning them into tools of personal expression.

Further Reading

Albright, Daniel. *Modernism and Music*. Chicago/London: University of Chicago Press, 2004.

Daniel Albright, Professor at Harvard University, collected various representative texts from composers—and some from other artists—which show the theorizing wanderings of the mind of composers who were much concerned about the "progress" of music. The notion of modernism is, in this informative book, taken much wider than in the present essay, including both music and sonic art. The sources make fascinating reading, giving an impression of a mental field covering a wide range between profound insights and utter nonsense. Albright treats "modernism" as a mentality, thus exposing the inner contradictions inevitable with the experimental thinking that was characteristic of this mentality.

Bacri, Nicolas. *Notes Étrangères*. Biaritz/Paris: Atlantica-Séguier, 2004.

A unique meditation written by a highly gifted composer upon his own artistic and philosophical development, from modernism to an expressive and personal traditionalism. Interestingly, Bacri does not reject modernism as such, and speaks with respect about his colleagues in "the other field," while questioning the fundaments of the conventional avant-garde. As a result, he feels an underlying tension between his new, expressive ideals and modernity as symbolized by modernism, and experiences this tension as a stimulus to creation.

Dorschel, Andreas, ed. *Gemurmel unterhalb des Rauschens: Theodor W. Adorno und Richard Strauss*. Vienna: Universal Edition, 2004.

The result of a symposium in which aesthetic value judgments were examined, especially in relation to Adorno's negative and unfair assessment of the music of Richard Strauss. A fascinating study of twentieth-century misconceptions of beauty, expression, and morality. Dorschel lectures at Stanford University and in Graz. As head of the Institute of Aesthetics at the Universität für Musik und Darstellende Kunst in Graz (Austria), Dorschel explores the ambiguous territory where artistic creation, philosophy, and broader cultural movements overlap (philosophy, aesthetics, history of ideas).

Dutton, Denis. *The Art Instinct: Beauty, Pleasure & Human Evolution*. New York: Bloomsbury Press, 2009.

This already famous book explores the deep connections between the ways humans create and consume art and the characteristics of our brains and behaviors that are rooted in evolutionary adaptations. Art—real art—is not a luxury bonus but forms an essential part of being human.

Eliot, T. S. "Tradition and the Individual Talent" (1920), in *The Sacred Wood and Major Early Essays*. Mineola: *Dover Publications*, 1997.

In this influential essay, Eliot challenges our common perception that a poet's greatness and individuality lie in his departure from his predecessors. Rather, Eliot argues that "the most individual parts of his (the poet's) work may be those in which the dead poets, his ancestors, assert their immortality most vigorously." He paints a virtual community of artists, bound by sympathy to common ideals, which leaves enough freedom for personal interpretation and in which comparable ambitions reinforce each other. An apt description of how a healthy and living tradition works. See also under Straus for a different picture.

Euron, Paulo. *Art, Beauty and Imitation: An Outline of Aesthetics*. Rome: Aracne, 2009.

This book is a historical introduction to the topic of aesthetics and presents some ideas of those philosophers that are a constitutive part of the contemporary experience of works of art and beauty. Our ideas about art and beauty are not only our individual and personal conceptions, but come from a millenarian tradition, even if we are not aware of it. Euron, who lectures at the University of Turin, deals with some essential philosophical questions related to our experience of artworks: what has art to do with truth, and with morality? Are works of art imitations of reality?

Finkielkraut, Alain. *The Defeat of the Mind*. New York: Columbia University Press, 1995. Original publication: Paris: Editions Gallimard, 1987.

In a provocative, philosophically grounded contribution to the current debate on multiculturalism, French thinker Finkielkraut maintains that the cultural relativism advanced by French anthropologist Claude Levi-Strauss and by Third World theorists such as Frantz Fanon has led to a contemporary "cult of difference" and to nationalist politics that exalt group identity over individual freedoms. Finkielkraut critiques the seductive perils of the nineteenth-century German model of the *Volk* (people), whereby the individual can join the nation only if he or she belongs to an ethnic group, and he detects reverberations of this line of thought in anticolonial, anti-Western attitudes and in the modern multicultural movement, with striking implications for the way in which the arts within Western civilization, and their values, are considered. An idea, born from postcolonial guilt, gradually became a self-destructive tool with which to attack individual artistic achievement as "elitist" and "antidemocratic."

Galey, Mathieu. *Les yeux ouverts*. Paris: Ed. Centurion, 1981.

A collection of touching interviews with Marguerite Yourcenar, comparable to De Rosbo's interview book, in which Yourcenar speaks about life, literature, culture, and all the ups and downs of her long and interesting journey through twentieth-century waters, as it were on a "ship" of both traditionally humanistic values and unconventional, personal ideas. Her independence from fashionable notions and superficial trends stamps both her books and the interviews with a timeless and authentic quality, which makes her voice contemporary forever.

Holloway, Robin. *Debussy and Wagner*. London: E. Eulenburg, 1979.

In this remarkable study, Holloway, a lecturer at Cambridge University and composer of music with one foot in modernism and the other in tradition, shows how much Debussy's life work is based upon a full and profound absorption of the music of Wagner. Given the fundamental differences in culture, character, and taste of the two composers, it shows how influences on a fundamental level can be transformed and given a very different artistic and expressive meaning. Reading this book in conjunction with the mentioned texts by Eliot and Straus reveals the psychology of digestion of influences and the overcoming of an undermining artistic "threat."

Nehamas, Alexander. *Only a Promise of Happiness: The Place of Beauty in a World of Art*. Princeton: Princeton University Press, 2007.

In this book, Alexander Nehamas reclaims beauty from its critics (artists, philosophers) who, in the twentieth century, suspected that beauty merely paints over or distracts us from horrors. He seeks to restore its place in art, to re-establish the connections among art, beauty, and desire, and to show that the values of art, independently of their moral worth, are equally crucial to the rest of life. Beauty can be "dangerous," but it touches at a profound, spiritual longing in the human soul, without which the development of the individual would be incomplete.

Painter, Karen. *Symphonic Aspirations, German Music and Politics 1900–1945*. Cambridge (Mass.): Harvard University Press, 2007.

An overview of the entanglement of high art music with German politics in a time when serious music occupied a central place in society as a symbol of both the general culture and the cultural identity of the nation, showing the dangers of the politization of art, which can thus become a tool of manipulation. This deplorable history is one of the many causes of the marginalization of classical music and the defamation of the classical tradition in the present.

Peyser, Joan. *Boulez*. New York: Schirmer Books, 1976.

A well-known but not uncontroversial biography in which the author, next to collecting facts about music and performances, tries to probe under the outward mask of this secretive sonic artist. Because Boulez is not a composer, and his music is never intended to relate to notions of musical meaning and expressiveness, it is only logical that he refused to share personal and private information, which, in his case, would not shed light upon his oeuvre anyway, or would be pointless to it. As Boulez said himself: "I will be the first composer who will not have a biography" (i.e., a biography in the usual sense of the term). Unintentionally, this attitude is quite revealing about Boulez's motivation and explains a lot about the nature of his work and its relation to the times.

Riemen, Rob. *Nobility of Spirit, a Forgotten Ideal*. New Haven and London: Yale University Press, 2008.

In the pages of this slim book, Riemen, founder of the influential Nexus Institute in the Netherlands, argues that nobility of spirit is the quintessence of a civilized world. It is, as Thomas Mann believed, the sole corrective for human history. Nobility of spirit is, as the book makes clear, a mentality, an approach to existential and cultural questions, a critical but aspirational frame of mind, always placing civilized values and the human quest for truth and the dignity of life at the center. Without nobility of spirit, culture vanishes, together with the sense of human development, and a free and democratic society becomes vulnerable to forces that seek to undermine it. When culture vanishes, the beginning of the end of civilization comes in sight. Yet in the early twenty-first century, a time when human dignity and freedom are imperilled, the concept of nobility of spirit (which is, in fact, the essence of Europe's age-old humanism) is seldom considered.

Rosbo, Patrick de. *Entretiens radiophoniques avec Marguerite Yourcenar*. Paris: Mercure de France, 1980.

In this collection of radio interviews, Marguerite Yourcenar talks about her oeuvre, explains her motivations, her methods, her views on life. The questions put by Patrick de Rosbo invite Yourcenar to get at the heart of her writings and of literature in general, offering insights in one of the greatest literary personalities of the 20th century who asserted a voice of intense but controlled classicism in a period of extreme diversity. After a rather marginal career in the Interbellum, she went to live in the USA in 1939, where in the 1950s she acquired world fame with her *Mémoires d'Hadrien* (1951), followed by its "counterpart" *L'Oeuvre au noir* (1968). Culturally she remained thoroughly French and entered, as the first woman in history, the Académie Française in 1980, which caused quite a stir in the French cultural world.

Ross, Alex: *The Rest Is Noise*. New York: Picador, 2007.

A most interesting and colorful history of twentieth-century music, not told in conventional terms of developments of the dynamics of the sound material, as it is so often presented, but as an art form profoundly connected with and influenced by personal, historical, and political circumstances. Its ironic and ambiguous title may refer to the distinction between music and sonic art, although Ross never affords himself a value judgment of the genres. Ross shows how the often inaccessible "modern music" of the last century should be listened to: as expression or reflection of human adventure, failure, endeavor, and achievement. As such, it is not difficult to understand the many misconceptions and tragedies that have destroyed music as a high art form and its place in society. Ross does not criticize the aberrations of modernism: the historical facts speak for themselves and create a fascinating story along the way. The only weakness of the book that may be pointed out is the lack of value distinction between high and low culture, which explains the respect with which Ross discusses the best and the worst in one breath, but that is a minor complaint in comparison with its brilliant achievement.

Roth, Ernst. *The Business of Music; Reflections of a Music Publisher*. London: Cassell, 1966.

The interesting memoirs of an interesting and erudite man, who, in 1922, entered the Viennese music publishing house of Universal Edition, where, from 1928 to 1938, he was head of the publications department. In 1938, he joined Boosey & Hawkes in London. He has been publisher, counselor, and friend to many distinguished composers like Stravinsky, Strauss, Bartok, Schönberg, Berg, and Webern. In writing about the new music of Boulez and Stockhausen and of the lesser innovators, he is forthright and outspoken, understanding from the professional's view the fragile relationship between the composer and his audiences. This book is in complete form on the internet: www.musicweb-international.com/ Roth/index.htm

Schultz, Wolfgang-Andreas. *Damit die Musik nicht aufhört*. Eisenach: Musikalienhandlung Karl Dieter Wagner, 1997.

It is hoped that this remarkable essay will be translated into English sometime in the future: it is another revealing history of twentieth-century music, now treated as a narrative of depth psychology: a brilliant and clear exposition of the undercurrents of all the musical developments in a confused culture and dangerous world. Against the background of an evolutionary theory of consciousness, Schultz shows how and why profound psychological and spiritual conflicts create a music which reflects the inner landscape of Europe's cultural suicide. Here is a profound thinker about music who combines brilliant scholarship and erudition with great musical sensitivity.

Schultz, Wolfgang-Andreas. "Avantgarde und Trauma–Die Musik des 20. Jahrhunderts und die Erfahrungen der Weltkriege," in: *Lettre International*, deutsche Ausgabe Nr. 71. Berlin, Winter 2005.

In this explorative and groundbreaking essay, Schultz shows the connection between the individual and collective experience of war trauma and ideas of avant-gardism in the twentieth century. The psychological similarities between traumatized war victims and the character of certain post-1918 and post-1945 works is striking and make the rupture of the European musical tradition understandable from the human point of view. Modernism developed under the pressure of profound inner conflicts and insoluble dilemmas caused by the industrialization and technologization of society and the politization of the musical world, but much more so by the shocks of war. As confirmed by the above-mentioned book of Alex Ross, twentieth-century music did not develop on an island of hermetic intellectualism; this façade was a defence mechanism for an utterly fragile aesthetic and psychological position.

Scruton, Roger. *The Aesthetics of Music.* Oxford: Oxford University Press, 1997.

A monumental tome in which both philosophical and psychological aspects of the art form find a clear and most readable expression, thanks to Scruton's mastery over language and razor-sharp analytical and synthetical intelligence. Problems of representation, understanding, expression, analysis, form, and performance receive a treatment which often seems definite; especially the chapters upon tonality and culture deserve the closest attention in relation to the revival of the classical tradition and its potential. In the chapter upon culture, Scruton invokes the need of a musical equivalent of T. S. Eliot's *Four Quartets*, a rediscovery of the tonal language, "which will also redeem the time," in contrast to the rather cheap minimalist tonalities which became so popular with those audiences for which high-art classical music is too difficult.

Scruton, Roger. *Modern Culture.* London and New York: *Continuum*, 1998.

In this thought-provoking book, Scruton argues for the spiritual origin of culture in all its forms and mounts a defence of Western high culture against its intellectual critics. He shows the emptiness and destructiveness of much modern thought, explains how avant-garde and kitsch are interrelated, and underlines the fundamental importance of education and traditional cultural values. One does not have to agree with Scruton's stress upon the importance of the community, the "tribe," in relation to the individual, to see how right he is when he shows that artistic originality can only exist against the background of a tradition. Also, his focus upon organized religion may be a bit much in the context, but it is clear that spirituality in any form lies at the heart of authentic artistic creation, to protect it from the eroding cynicism which in our time is represented by "the market."

Scruton, Roger. *Understanding Music.* London and New York: *Continuum*, 2009.

The sequel to *The Aesthetics of Music*, in the form of a collection of wide-ranging essays on all aspects of the theory and practice of music, presenting a powerful encomium of the European classical tradition and showing the connection of music with the moral life. To link high-art music with morality may seem, at first sight, a bit far-fetched; but if one realizes that in the visual arts and in music—in the process of developing the capacity of discernment—one makes value judgments all the time, the connection becomes clearer. Music influences our inner life and thus brings up the matter of morality and judgment with every work that tells us something about ourselves. Scruton is much more than a philosopher: he is a cultural prophet, and the accumulation of insights he offers in any publication is a continuous stimulus to further exploration and discussion.

Steiner, George. *In Bluebeard's Castle: Some Notes Toward the Redefinition of Culture.* London: Faber & Faber, 1971.

Steiner's central obsession in his oeuvre is the Holocaust, and specifically the idea that the Holocaust's ashes spread from high culture's Promethean fire: that the civilization which produced Bach also produced Buchenwald. This book is an attempt at a broad analysis of the cultural erosion of the last century by an erudite cultural philosopher—first confirming that the twentieth-century angst is justified and that much which was a precious treasure has been lost, then encouraging us to surrender to modernity and try to make the best of it. Steiner tries to make credible the idea that the Holocaust is the logical and inevitable result of structural evil at the heart of European civilization, instead of the usual incapacity of man to live up to his own ideals, implicitly blaming the spirit that created high culture for the crimes committed by people who were too primitive to understand it. The book unintentionally offers an apt explanation of the deeper motivation of postwar modernism: the abhorrence of its own inherited culture.

Storr, Anthony. *Music and the Mind.* London: Harper Collins Publishers, 1992.

Storr believes that, today, music is a deeply significant experience for a greater number of people that ever before. In this challenging book, he explores why this should be so. Drawing on a wide variety of opinions, Storr argues that the patterns of music make sense of our inner experience, giving both structure and coherence to our emotional life. It is because music possesses this capacity to restore our sense of personal wholeness, in a culture which requires us to separate rational thought from feelings, that many people find it so life enhancing.

Straus, Joseph N. *Remaking the Past: Musical Modernism and the Influence of the Tonal Tradition.* Cambridge (Mass.): Harvard University Press, 1990.

Straus details the revisionary strategies of some twentieth-century composers (Stravinsky, Bartok, Schönberg, Berg, Webern) and how they transformed concepts of the tonal tradition in creating their radically new sonorities and structures. He defines what he sees as early modernism as shaped by the aggressive reinterpretation of eighteenth- and nineteenth-century models. Straus' provocative but sensible ideas are based largely on literary critic Harold Bloom's concept of "misreading"—not a failed reading, but one in which a poet asserts his or her artistic voice by confronting, struggling with, and ultimately overcoming the influence of a predecessor. This is a relationship quite different from the one described by T. S. Eliot in his *Tradition and the Individual Talent*, and shows the innate hostility toward tradition born from insecurity, which is symptomatic of a period following a culmination of artistic achievement.

Taruskin, Richard. *Stravinsky and the Russian Traditions.* Berkeley, Los Angeles and London: University of California Press, 1996

Stravinsky underplayed his Russian past in favor of a European cosmopolitanism but Taruskin has refused to take the composer at his word. He defines Stravinsky's relationship to the musical and artistic traditions of his native land and gives a dramatically new picture of one of the major figures in the history of music. Taruskin demonstrates how Stravinsky achieved his technique by combining what was most characteristically Russian in his musical training with stylistic elements abstracted from Russian folklore. The stylistic synthesis thus achieved formed Stravinsky as a composer for life, whatever the aesthetic allegiances he later professed, and shows the various ways in which a tradition can define even the most unexpected musical surfaces.

Thacker, Toby. *Music after Hitler, 1945–1955.* Aldershot (UK) and Burlington (USA): Ashgate Publishing Ltd., 2007.

A thorough study of the ten years of Allied occupation of Germany when its musical life, which was deemed important in the context of reorientation of society, was reorganized, with the inevitable development during the first years of the Cold War of the schism between western and eastern zones and their respective music policies. Now so many archives have been opened to research, it appears that postwar modernism in the West (especially West Germany) was as politically charged as musical culture under the Soviet regime, presenting a mirror image of totalitarian thought in two different society types.

Tzonis, Alexander and Lefaivre, Liane. *Classical Architecture: The Poetics of Order.* Cambridge (Mass.): Massachusetts Institute of Technology, 1986.
   A most instructive visual demonstration of how a cultural tradition works: classical architecture is not treated as a history of designs, but as a continuum of ideas which find different realization in different periods and circumstances, and in the hands of different personalities. The book, amply enlivened with beautiful illustrations and architectural designs, researches the generative rules, the poetics of composition that classical architecture shares with classical music, poetry, and drama. It demonstrates how the multiple attempts to create a structure which embodies humanistic and civilizational values, and that attempts to overcome inner contradictions, result in a continuous tension between the ideal and the real which stimulates ever new variations and interpretations. As a metaphor for a new, classical tradition this book is a fundamental text.

Ward-Perkins, Bryan. *The Fall of Rome and the End of Civilization.* Oxford: Oxford University Press, 2005.
   The author encourages the reader to reconsider modern-day complacency by reclaiming the drama and violence of the last days of the Roman world and reminding us of the very real difficulties that the peoples of the empire faced in adjusting to the invaders' rule. He examines the reasons for the disintegration of the Roman world to a society where living standards collapsed to prehistoric levels. For our own time this story is still significant, since it shows the importance of maintaining cultural values as the center of a civilization, even when erosion takes place at the margins. Cultural disintegration heralds wider erosion and results in vulnerability to hostile forces, both inside and outside of society.

Wittkower, Rudolf. *Architectural Principles in the Age of Humanism.* London: Academy Editions, 1988 and New York: St. Martin's Press, 1988.
   Comparable to Tzonis/Lefaivre's *Classical Architecture* as a demonstration of how a tradition functions, but focusing upon Renaissance interpretation of concepts of antiquity. Particularly interesting are the examples from Alberti's and Palladio's works, which are the result of a strong orientation upon antique examples but show a striking originality. The chapters upon so-called "harmonic proportion" link architectural design to music, which throws light upon the mimetic aspects of proportion and relationships that underlie all classical art.

Yourcenar, Marguerite. *Mémoires d'Hadrien*. Paris: Gallimard, 1951/2005.

This celebrated novel presents a vision of a world, of a society, where all determining factors and forces would be in harmony with each other, where a strong notion of civilization would be the framework within which different peoples, different cultures, could flourish. It would be a fundamentally traditional society where examples of excellence and the results of experience would be all-important. Rome was a Hellenistic culture, continuously turning to Greece for its inspiration and trying to create monuments that embodied its values and which would last through the centuries. But Yourcenar also shows how fragile such balance is, how much effort and patience has to be invested to achieve some equilibrium, and how easily cracks appear in the beautiful surface.

Index of Names

Index of Subjects

anosognosia, collective, 50
architecture, classical, 73–75
avantgarde and trauma, 43

Bubbles (the Bubbles hoax), x

cultural identity, xviii, xix, xxiii, 1–2,
   49, 75, 82, 85, 89, 100, 111, 112, 114,
   123, 133
cultural relativism, 90, 91–93, 94, 113,
   114, 132

Darmstadt summer course, 33
dodecaphony, 24, 29, 30, 32, 33
Donaueschingen Festival, 32, 33
Dutch modern music establishment, x

education, 102–104
European malaise, xv–xvii, xix, 1, 2

functionality, architectural, 72

German modernism, 99–101
government cuts in the arts, xiii

IRCAM, 63

Khakheperresenb's complaint, 66

kitsch, 4–6, 7–8, 9, 15, 71, 73, 88, 121,
   136

magical square, 29
mimetic thinking, 19–21
modernist revolution, Netherlands, in
   the, ix

neuroscience, 44–46

originality, 66, 102, 104

painting, figurative, 6, 15, 17, 73, 105,
   112
Pirahas, 84, 94
postmodern, postmodernism, 1, 3, 19,
   73, 82, 94, 108, 109, 114
process music, 3

Renaissance, Augustan, 116
Renaissance, Italian, xxii, 10

serialism, 24, 29, 31, 58, 87

universal civilizational values, 91–93

virtual space of music, 39–41

Wagnerism, 35

About the Author

John Borstlap (b. 1950) studied at the Rotterdam Conservatory and received a master's degree from the University of Cambridge, England. His *Violin Concerto* won prizes at the Prince Pierre Competition in Monaco and the Wieniawski Competition in Poznan, Poland. He has also received commissions from various institutions, including the Johan Wagenaar Foundation, the Dutch government, and the Culture Company.

His chamber music is performed in the Netherlands and abroad and has been recorded for radio broadcasts. Performances of his *Sinfonia* in 1990 by the Netherlands Chamber Orchestra under Hartmut Haenchen, established John Borstlap's reputation as a distinctive orchestral composer of classically orientated music. A collection of his chamber works was recorded as *Hyperion's Dream*, Albany Records in 1997. His compositions have been performed by, among others, the New Queen's Hall Orchestra in London, the Netherlands Symphony Orchestra, the Netherlands Chamber Orchestra, and the Orchestre National de Montpellier.

John Borstlap has also authored articles on contemporary music and other cultural issues, organized and partook in academic music conferences and organized a music festival. Together with two collegues, he founded the Composers Group Amsterdam, which appeared on Dutch national TV and on German national radio. www.johnborstlap.com.